Landscapes of

Hugh Brody is a writer, anthropo[...]
publishing *Inishkillane*, his classic study of the west of [...]
he spent many years immersed in communities of indigenous
peoples of Arctic and sub-Arctic Canada. His books include
The People's Land, *Maps and Dreams*, *The Other Side of Eden* and
a collection of short stories, *Means of Escape*. His films include
Nineteen Nineteen, starring Paul Scofield and Maria Schell, and
a series of documentaries made in the Canadian north. He also
directed *Tracks Across Sand*, a set of films made with the
‡Khomani San of the southern Kalahari.

Further praise for *Landscapes of Silence*:

'A wonderfully vivid and honest work that is simultaneously anthropology, autobiography, and philosophy.' James Cullingham,
author, film-maker and journalist

'Brody learns how the well-being of the Inuit is inseparable from
that of humanity . . . Capitalism and its colonial frontiers, he writes,
'are just one version of humanity'. There are other stories and realities to listen to, for silence to become song. In this book we hear
that song.' Elizabeth Wainwright, *Geographical*

'We have a teaching where I come from that when we speak,
our Ancestors hear us. This book must soothe the shattering silences that Hugh Brody's many ancestors, and mine, endured.
I deeply identify with his journey of yearning, of sorrow, and,
ultimately, of interwoven connections and belonging. Every
reflection is brought forward from the past and connected to a current truth in each of us.' Jada-Gabrielle Pape, Coast Salish from
the Saanich and Snuneymuxw Nations, certified grief and trauma
counsellor

'Hugh Brody has crafted a unique, harrowing and always luminous journey of discovery into his own past, its traumas and whispers, relating those personal experiences of suppression with the way in which colonised people around the world have been abused, and yet he's managed to break the ice of silence and reach our interconnected hearts.' Ariel Dorfman

'A challenging and absorbing read, not to be missed.' Peter J. Usher, author of *Joey Jacobson's War*

'A powerful piece of writing, and it does such a wonderful job of pulling together divergent strands into something that feels so much bigger than itself. It's brave, honest, and beautiful . . . ' Adam Weymouth, author of *Kings of the Yukon*

---

by the same author

BOOKS

Gola: The Life and Last Days of an Island Community (with F. H. A. Aalen)
Indians On Skid Row
Inishkillane
The People's Land
Maps and Dreams
Living Arctic
Means of Escape
The Other Side of Eden

FILMS

The People's Land (with Michael Grigsby)
Treaty 8 Country (with Anne Cubitt)
People of the Islands
Nineteen Nineteen (with Michael Ignatieff)
On Indian Land
Hunters and Bombers (with Nigel Markham)
Time Immemorial
The Washing of Tears
England's Henry Moore (with Anthony Barnett)
Inside Australia with Antony Gormley
The Meaning of Life
Tracks Across Sand

HUGH BRODY

LANDSCAPES *of* SILENCE

From Childhood to the Arctic

First published in the UK and the USA in 2022
by Faber & Faber Ltd
The Bindery, 51 Hatton Garden
London ECIN 8HN

Typeset by Paul Baillie-Lane
Printed and bound in the UK by CPI Group (UK) Ltd, Croydon CRO 4YY

A CIP record for this book
is available from the British Library

ISBN 978–0–571–37094–8

Printed and bound in the UK on FSC® certified paper in line with our continuing
commitment to ethical business practices, sustainability and the environment.
For further information see faber.co.uk/environmental-policy

10 9 8 7 6 5 4 3 2 1

For Tomo Brody
1983–2020

CONTENTS

BEFORE THE BEGINNING

qanik	falling snow
aputi	snow lying as a covering on the ground
maujaq	soft snow that you sink into and struggle to travel through
masak	snow on the ground that has become wet
mannguq	snow half thawed or mixed with water (e.g. for building up sledge runners)
sitilluqaaq	the hardest, wind-driven crystalline snow
auvik	a block of snow cut from a snowdrift to use for igloo building
igluvigaksaq	snow that is good for making an igloo
pukak	snow that is in granules, found on grassy land, underneath newer snow, especially useful for melting into water
minguliq	fine, powdery snow that has made its way through cracks around doors or windows
natiruvaq	snow that is blown by the wind and builds up inside a doorway
piruriniq	snow that has piled up on an object
aniuk	an isolated, shaded patch of snow that has stayed frozen into summer

These are some of the many words for snow in Inuktitut, the language of the Inuit, the hunters and gatherers of the eastern Arctic.

Try reading them out loud. No matter that you may not know how to pronounce those unfamiliar combinations of letters – though it is helpful to know that 'q' at the end of a word is a voiced sound just below the place at the back of the mouth where we make the letter 'k'. To read these words, even without knowing how Inuktitut sounds, is to hear that each of them is its own specific term. No two of them seem to be related. Every bit of that world of snows is its own piece of language, a separate part of the world that Inuit encounter and know. A grid of their way of seeing the land and being in it, laid onto a territory often made up of snow.

So how many words do the Inuit have for snow? As you can see and hear in that list of different sounds, the answer is none. There is no word for the cold white stuff we call 'snow'; only the many words for the multitude of different forms snow can take, each one specific. For the same deep reasons, there is no word for 'seal', the animal; instead, everyone must say what has been seen, must use and share detailed, specific knowledge. This is a world, a mind, in which generalities and categories are avoided. In the same way, it is a language that, before the arrival of European influences, did not count beyond the number five. Later I would discover that these features of Inuktitut are to be found in hunter-gatherer languages around the world.

I spent some ten years living and working in the Canadian north, and for the first two of those years was able to spend much of my time learning two Inuktitut dialects. I was travelling in my mind, with the sounds I began to be able to shape, into somewhere very far from anywhere I had ever been. And to the very place I most had wanted to be – though I would not have been able to say why. As I learned the words for snow, I learned also that there is a whole other way of hearing and sustaining knowledge, and, most important of all, that the wellbeing of the Inuit might be inseparable from the wellbeing of humanity.

———————

This book is an attempt to understand how I came to make that journey into the far north. I have been wonderfully fortunate to have spent long periods deep within the lives and lands of those inspiring people. While there, and when bringing back memories of those journeys, I could to some extent ignore all the things that came from outside, and be absorbed into the aspects of mind that originated in the north: language, memories, stories.

But in the end it was not possible to disregard the implications of the outside influences, and, the more I listened, and the more people talked with me, the more I came to understand that even here, many hundreds of miles from a road, factory or any aspect of urban development, the people were suffering from the dominant forces of outsider power, and were facing both the threat and first realities of dispossession. Yet, with a paradoxical force, the more people talked to me, sharing what they had experienced and how they felt, the more I began to realise that despite the continuity of storytelling and voices of political protest, there was a layer of silence.

———————

Along with many hundreds of other indigenous languages, Inuktitut is at risk. Across much of the Arctic it is no longer spoken, and even where it continues to be the language of the home, English tends to be dominant. At the same time, the elders whose

3

role has been to sustain both language and indigenous narratives are becoming fewer and less sure of their own authority. The process of imperialism, with its insistence on new forms of religious belief, schooling and economic order, creates and then comes to depend on this deep and deepening silence.

Thus silence is allied to dispossession. Those who have lost their lands can no longer tell their stories; those whose stories have been silenced can no longer sustain the land. Those who have denied or subverted the rights of others insist that those others have nothing of any importance to say. They themselves, the conquerors and thieves, do not want history to be heard.

Wherever I have lived and worked as an anthropologist or film-maker I have found this alliance of dispossession and silence. Again and again, from villages in the west of Ireland to communities in western India to the Kalahari desert to many regions of the Canadian north, I have been shown the double need both to listen and to support those who resist dispossession. This book has grown from a realisation that there was always a thread that connected this flow of work and my own formation. So a question came to mind: why was I, a boy from the suburbs of a city in the north of England, drawn to remote edges of the world?

Anthropologists often go to the edges of their world, expecting to find the meaning of a society and, without always acknowledging it, the meaning of their discipline and themselves. I too went to the edges, and discovered both the heart of other ways of living and, to my surprise, also learned that by going to the edge we can discover what lies at the centre. The purposes, beliefs, morality and even the character of a society reveal themselves when it claims a frontier. Indigenous and tribal peoples, for whom our frontiers are their homelands, witness and suffer the consequences. And it is possible to see, at seemingly distant frontiers, that the human condition can be rethought and transformed, away from abuse, towards respect for where we live and for one another.

I was brought up in the aftermath of the Second World War, living a childhood in which the Nazis and mass murder were half hidden but always present, in a Jewish family that was riven by worries that it might or might not belong. I had to escape the shadows, the uncertainties. It did not, at first, have to be very far – a three-mile bike ride up the road from a suburban home to the Derbyshire moors was an early journey to another kind of place; later it was further afield – to more distant parts of the English countryside, then to Israel, Ireland and, at last, to the Canadian high Arctic. At each version of elsewhere I found both edges and, more and more to my surprise, the nature of the centres I thought I was leaving behind.

As I wrote about this childhood and the journeys that came from escaping it, I wondered if I was also writing an anthropology of myself. This book depends on a selection of the moments, a choice of episodes and stories that seem to me to speak to ideas from my life. Here are recollections and anthropological journeys that raise questions about something of much greater interest.

I do not want to suggest that I knew from the start, or had in mind all the way along, what this set of memories and findings would mean. In reality, as is so often the case with both writing and making films, as I travelled in the work, I navigated my way towards connections that I had not known, or did not know that I had known, when I set out.

There is a sequence of stories that I return to here. The resonances of the Holocaust in a suburban home, a passion for collecting birds' eggs, a family that sought acceptance yet lived in relation to some other, but lost, part of European history, a journey of discovery to Palestine and Israel, and then, at last, the escape to the Arctic. This book is a collage of those journeys. Within each part I found silences. Many kinds of silence. And always the question of where it came from and what purposes it served. In each place I find an intersection, or a confluence, where dispossession and displacement join forces with reluctance or inability to speak out, to own up to what is most pressingly real. And in each place, within each layer of this book, there are narratives of abuse – of people, because of their supposed racial difference, and of the land.

All writing is to some degree a reckoning with oneself. Writers both start and stop what they do because, from within themselves, they know they have to; it may be years, or never, before they know where the writing originated or what it was really about. So I may only be guessing, or staying too close to the surface, when I say that this book, for now, has come from troubled silences, the depths of both public and private history, and recurrent forms and consequences of dispossession, alongside a wish to tell a set of stories that are both anthropology and myself.

I have wanted to allow the voices of those I met and learned from to guide what I say, to show what I have learned. This telling of stories, looking to memories and anecdotes, has always been at the heart of my work as an anthropologist and film-maker. The truths of anthropology, I am sure, reveal themselves in the stories of others. But here the stories are for the most part my own. Yet this is only a partial memoir. I follow episodes in my own life, but many phases of my life and work have no place in the themes here. Rather, I select the episodes, the anecdotes and memories, because they seem to me to reveal something larger and more compelling than the particular narrative of my own life. Through them I hope that I can throw some light onto places where darkness has caused, and continues to cause, immeasurable harm. In this way I hope that I can do some much needed justice to the stories that are among the heartlands of our time.

I have been writing the last pieces of this book as the Covid-19 pandemic has been raging around the world. The anguish and fear have been filling my head and heart. Loved ones at risk at home, and the terrible danger for peoples who live at the edges of the world. The virus leaps across oceans, forests and Arctic ice-fields, carried by the crews and passengers of aeroplanes that connect the most remote frontier with urban centres. The people at the edges, often provided with minimal medical facilities and living in crowded households with limited sanitation, are at maximum risk. Some of the most telling ironies of modernity are being revealed: great wealth, at the centre, controls the planes, brings 'development', while those who are supposed to benefit from this 'development', living in modern forms of poverty, are especially vulnerable to the disease. The forces that give rise to and then seek to eliminate Covid-19 are closely allied to the forces that devastate indigenous peoples. I dread the news.

I have wondered if this lurch in the fate of the world should cause me to rethink what I have written here. But this book is built with events and memories along the way to an appreciation of what it is, or can be, to be human. Here, I hope, is a journey, or set of journeys, that can both see and move away from the shadow of death.

The sounds of the words for snow, along with the wealth of meaning and knowledge carried in those sounds, are both poetry and wisdom for humanity. The disappearance of such knowledge and meaning, the failure to tell the stories, the loss of the land where the stories belong, is where silence and dispossession converge. Having spoken some of the Inuktitut words, I hope that you will be able to travel back to where I learned about both dispossession and silence, and along some of the routes that are surprisingly but deeply connected by those two dangerous, often deadly, realities.

TO START

It was late in the evening, at the end of July 2009. I was standing in a line at Heathrow Airport waiting to board a flight to Cape Town, on my way to the southern Kalahari. I was thinking about, remembering, anticipating the rolling red sand dunes and dry river beds of the Northern Cape, where the borders of South Africa, Namibia and Botswana meet. I had been many times before, working with Bushman families, the people who had been known as the ‡Khomani San. This was a return, near the end of a long series of projects aimed at discovering what could possibly compensate these survivors for the identity, dignity and resources that had been progressively undermined and taken from them by the arrival of aggressive settlers on their lands. I had been listening to oral histories, making maps, filming journeys back to places in the desert where the Bushmen had once lived. Hearing about extreme loss and dispossession, and building a recovery of heritage and home; challenging the silences. Though it is easier to secure justice than to achieve wellbeing.

I was almost at the door to the plane. My phone rang. It was news about my mother: she had fallen, hit her head, was unconscious. I should call the hospital and my brother. I continued into the crowded plane, and sat down in a middle seat. I leant forward to be as out of sight as possible of any cabin crew, held the phone to my ear, covered it with my hand and, as we taxied down the runway then lurched up into the sky, I made call after call. I learned that my mother had crashed down beside a small table, hitting her head hard on its edge. There was a remote possibility that she could be operated on, and perhaps brought back to consciousness. But she had always opposed resuscitation, had even written a letter to her solicitor to say as much. So we decided, over the phone, in a triangle of calls between Sheffield where she was lying in a hospital bed, the Midwest of America where my brother was living, and the plane climbing above the earth en route from London to Africa, that there should be no surgery, no attempt to save her life.

I flew back to London the following night and made my way to the hospital in Sheffield. Some of the family were already there, staying with her. I joined them. For most of the time she lay very still, eyes closed, and then sudden lurches of facial movement, her eyes fluttering open and shut, and gasping sounds coming from her throat, as if in some despairing attempt to surface, failing, and sinking back. Her lips were dry, parched and cracking. She was given no nourishment or treatment of any kind. She had been marked as 'do not resuscitate'. Shouldn't she be given fluids intravenously? Some pain relief – who was to know if she was suffering? No, said the nurses, there would be no pain, only deep unconsciousness, and if they were to administer fluids she could go on like this for many weeks. Each time she lurched and gasped, I wanted to protest, and kept asking that some kind of relief be administered, and was told again that this is what 'do not resuscitate' meant.

She lived like this, in supposed painless agony, for a week. I sat with her through much of what turned out to be her last night, feeling grief and, to my surprise and relief, surges of uncomplicated love. She was almost ninety-one, at the end of a life that had been riven with difficulties – both from the world and within herself. Many of these had been passed on to me, and to my relationship with her. Until that last night I don't think I ever thought I loved her, and she never had been able to speak or show her love for me. There was too much darkness, unspoken pain. I stayed sitting with her in the morning, watching her face, still impressive for its forceful beauty. At about 10 a.m. she gave a last shudder, a gasp, and died.

After the funeral I stayed for a week in her house, and began to go through files that she had kept in a cabinet at the back of a coat and broom cupboard, and a small cache of ancient cardboard boxes hidden away behind a high shelf piled with bedding. A trail of old letters, out-of-date passports, bank statements, records of events that had been stored because they were 'important papers' – things that must not be thrown out. I kept thinking that my mother would not have cared if my brother and I chucked the whole lot away without bothering to look at any of it. I imagined what she would have done if it were she who had the job of going through all these old family documents: my most convincing image was of her taking a few quick looks and then, with a sigh and a muttered expletive, throwing it all into a skip. But I was curious, wanting to have moments of connection with at least some of what had been kept for so many years, for the most part far out of sight.

I spent several days going through these papers, sometimes staring at them as if they were icons with surprising power, sometimes reading through them to find out what, after all, was reality. Often I was reminded of how little we had been told, how much was kept unspoken and unexplained. Many letters were searing reminders of how great the distance had been

between me and my family. So much that had never been said – be it the warmth and care that children need from parents and, indeed, that parents delight in from their children, or the details of all that my mother had lost, and the pointers to the forces of history by which she had been displaced, dispossessed, internally devastated.

Most poignant of all were the contents of the old boxes from behind the bedding. One of them contained a tiny silk embroidered dress, made for a baby but looking as if it had never been worn. A thing of strange beauty, from some other far-off world. Was this the first dress my mother had worn in the weeks after she was born, in Vienna, ninety years before? Or the dress that she had prepared for a child, a baby girl, who had died before I was born, and about whom she had almost never spoken? I felt a double sense of loss: if only she had been able to talk about it all, her life and losses, everything, and now there was no way I could ask her what this elegant little dress might mean.

The largest of the boxes contained a huge linen tablecloth, its edges ornamented with embroidery. It was for a table at which twenty people could have dined. This must have come from her childhood apartment, or her grandparents' home, in Austria or Poland. I would never know which. But there were other glimpses among her papers of what that home, or those homes, might have been like – signs and residue of loss. Documents that referred to houses and land in and around Lvov; the title deeds to oil fields in Poland; markers of all that had once been theirs, but was taken, lost, left behind.

My mother never mourned the losses. She had no apparent sense of the family's dispossession. She liked objects, and had carried with her to England some sets of beautiful china and that elusive quality that is called good taste. But she never ever suggested that the theft of property or the disappearance of potential wealth had any great significance for her. It was the killings, the shadows of murder, that hung over her, that she wanted to bury in silence and forgetting, but could not avoid transferring, could not conceal.

After my mother's house had been sold, and when at last it was empty of everything that had been hers, I made a final visit, to hand over the keys, to make sure we had not left anything behind. I stood in the kitchen and looked across the row of houses on the other side of the street and out towards the Derbyshire hills. And I felt a sadness that came from so far within me that I thought I was going to collapse.

My mother's house, the Derbyshire hills, a cabinet full of old papers, ancient cardboard boxes – all that I crossed the world to get away from, yet still so embedded within me. The home that hunts us down. The juxtaposition of silence and dispossession; a tangle of connections between where I came from and where I went to. This was a set of stories I knew I would have to find a way of telling.

———————

I spent two years learning Inuktitut. I often thought, as I struggled to make sense, that my teachers took time over my lessons, and showed such patience with my mistakes, because it gave them great entertainment – they would fall about laughing at the absurdities that came out of my mouth. There were many linguistic risks:

uuttuq	a seal lying out on the ice
uttuuk	a vagina
usuk	a penis
uujuq	boiled meat
ugjuq	a bearded seal
igjuuk	testicles
iijujuq	the Old Testament

My most important teacher, Simon Anaviapik, took obvious pride in reversing the usual colonial relationship: here was a white man from the south who was not in the north to trade, impose laws, teach or spread the word of God. I lived with an Inuit family, but I knew nothing of all that mattered most. Anaviapik took on the job of making sure I knew how to behave, what to believe and, above all, how to speak. Lessons would last through much of every night, and whenever possible, hunters took me out onto the land.

One day, after about a year of this immersion in Inuktitut, Anaviapik asked me why I thought he and others wanted me to learn their language, their way of being in the world. I did not say that it might be because it was a source of endless fun, as I confused stew with a penis; nor did I attempt to speak about the nature of colonial relationships. But Anaviapik wanted to give me *his* answer to his question: they were teaching me Inuktitut, he said, because they wanted me to speak for them. If the white people who dominated the world had the facts, knew more of what Anaviapik knew, and were given the truth, then many great injustices would be impossible. For him, the cruelty in history came from ignorance, from the failure to hear and be heard. Anaviapik believed – as many indigenous peoples believe – that if only those with the power understood them, then there would be an end to injustice and to any idea that the land did not belong to those who had lived on it since time immemorial. So I must be taught enough to be able to displace ignorance, to make Inuit experience and knowledge visible, and, in effect, to help break the silences in which he and his people so often had felt trapped.

This was forty years ago. Since then the Inuit have been well able to speak for themselves; of course they were able to speak for themselves then, too, but they were not heard.

I accepted and took advantage of my teachers' patience and their determination to have me learn. I was aware that no amount of thanks for all they gave me would be enough, but I could reassure myself that by learning as well as I could, and then working on land rights and cultural heritage projects on behalf of the Inuit and other peoples facing the same injustices, that I was in some way, to some extent, paying my dues. Yet there has always been another source of unease, another issue of obligation.

Anthropologists write or make films about other peoples. Often they have done this almost as if they the observers were not there, or nothing more than just another person, watching and listening but neutral and irrelevant. This concealing of the observer was challenged in the 1960s and '70s, leading to a more open form of anthropological writing and film-making, where the voice and presence of the observer is part of what is on record. In my own writing about other peoples I included myself in the frame to be sure that the reality of a relationship between me and those I wrote about was acknowledged. But it was without real balance: I gave snippets of my own story as part of the story that was the anthropology; meanwhile I felt free to describe the people I was working with in as much detail as possible, reaching as far back in time and deep into their lives as I thought would be interesting or helpful.

Even in acknowledging that I was present, I revealed a bare minimum of myself. This seemed appropriate, a recognition that what mattered was them, not me, but it could be said to be a convenient screening of myself while I was busy exposing others.

I have always disliked the narrator in films, the voice that takes ownership of the story, a voice that has so often been that of a white, middle-class male. The voice that knows everything, and speaks the right language, rendering the people in the film as strange and quaint and, hence, interesting, implying or even asserting that they are so very much in need of translation. A voice that itself sounds like another colonial project, the taking over of the subject of the film the way colonial powers take over the lands and lives of other people, making themselves rich and the people poor.

Narrated documentary can thus obscure and silence its subjects. I was always determined that my work would aim to do the opposite, and give people who have tended to be obscured and silenced a place in history and a voice in the world. Not through my definition of them but, if it were possible, through their definition of themselves. In the west of Ireland, on the North Pacific Coast, in western India and southern Africa people have taken me on journeys across their land and into their lives. I have listened and then had the job of making what I have heard and seen into books and films that are both about them and for them. Many voices, many kinds of history – but always theirs, not mine.

———————

It is over twenty years since I wrote *The Other Side of Eden*, which I thought would be my last attempt to put together what living with hunting peoples had taught me. In those intervening years I have spent time in western Canada and southern Africa, again hearing about the way colonial occupation and aggression have threatened whole communities with the loss of their lands, cultures and languages. And I kept thinking that if I were to write again about other people, I should begin by writing about myself. Something about the death of my mother, the papers and memorabilia she had kept hidden, the realisation that I had never understood why I fled the landscape of childhood, yet remained so deeply attached to it. Death closes history, and, at the same time, through a blend of loss and opportunity, opens it up. Or opens up the internal voices, the elusive memories.

But when it came to something that might be mere autobiography, I recoiled. For a long time I was frozen in my tracks. At the same time, I realised that I could not write yet again about others and not disclose who I am. I began to look at my own life and history, to think about the forces that shaped me as I grew up in a particular kind of home at a particular time. I understood that I was dealing with many zones of both personal difficulty and what might be called the wounds of history. I also began to discover that geographical distances dissolved in the light of internal, perhaps inseparable connection.

I left school as soon as I possibly could, without any idea of what came next. My university applications had disappeared into nowhere – some rejections, I think, some silences. I was not waiting to hear which university I might go to, even though my brother was at Oxford. I had little expectation of going to any university – there was no academic subject I wanted to study. I had a passion for the natural world but, having taken no science at school, this seemed to lead to no kind of career. If I thought about the future at all, it was with a fear of its being blank. I had said I would like to go to an art college. There were some conversations about the future, and the ridiculous idea emerged that I should become a chartered accountant. An eighteen year old whose interests were the countryside, birds, fishing and painting was to be an accountant? The rationale, if it deserves the word, came from an influential family friend: he thought it would be good if I became an accountant and then worked in his family firm, making a useful contribution to the avoidance of taxes.

I had nothing with which to oppose this strange idea since there was nothing I wanted to do that was deemed to have any link with earning a living. No one ever suggested that I take some time to puzzle it out. In this narrow view of life and its opportunities my parents were not much different from most of their generation: art school, birdwatching, the countryside – these may offer interesting hobbies, but nothing else. As for my inability to think beyond the narrow view of the times: well, I was part of those times too, and I suspect I was suffering from deep confusion. All I was sure about was that I had left *that* school: for some years after I would imagine, and even prepare, a plan for burning down the boarding house I had been in. But I also was aware that I was now back in Sheffield, at home with my parents and grandmother, returned full time to childhood territories of home. This was not a source of happiness, either to me or, in particular, my mother. She would slip back into reproachful anger towards me: I was such a disappointment to her. So I retreated to the top floor of the house, the two rooms of the attic, where I set up somewhere to paint, a record player to listen to a collection of old 78s I had discovered (with much Sibelius and Rachmaninov) and my books in the bedroom. If I was at home, I would be up in the attic.

So at the beginning of September of the year I left school I began work as an articled clerk in a firm of Sheffield accountants. The week before I began, my father took me to a large department store to buy me two suits – one dark grey, the other pale and mottled grey. From school uniform I already had white shirts, ties and black shoes. My life as an adult was to begin.

I found myself in an office where no one was allowed to use either a first name or a calculator. Dressed in suit and tie, aching with boredom and more and more eaten into by the acids of depression, being sure to call my fellow sufferers (I assumed they all suffered: how could they not?) Mr This and Miss That, I spent all of every day adding up columns of figures, noting the totals, then adding them again to check if it came out the same twice. Then adding them up again if they did not. Pounds, shillings and pence. Not even the simplicity of decimal currency. 240 pence to a pound; 12 pence to a shilling; three half crowns making seven and six; and the occasional guinea (because some professionals whose accounts we summed still charged fees in guineas). Lines and lines of three-columned numbers. Pages and pages of columns. Hours and hours of adding. It might have been a joy to subtract something, or have the excitement of long division. Adding and adding. Day after day. Weeks of this.

By the end of October I was wretched beyond wretchedness. In the evenings I escaped more and more to the attic. If I had dared be myself, I might have called it a studio. I felt it to be a generous crawl-hole where I hid from them all – not knowing who *they* all were – and had charcoal and paints, and where at that time, in those weeks of adding numbers, I painted a mural on a stretch of wall above a long window. I created a forest of trees among which foxes appeared, all in dark inks on white plaster: trees that were impenetrable and the foxes in profile, moving and standing among them. I liked the formalised, quick-inked shapes, and yet I believed that this work had no merit, would before long be painted over. I felt I was damaging the plaster, making a mess of it. I think now it may have been quite beautiful, haunting for the story it told about a forest and the life it contained, and the sense it must have given of the sadness of the boy who made that work. It was my answer, the only answer that my internal self could make, to the columns of numbers.

Each day, after the hours with the accounts, dressed in one of the two suits of my adult life, I walked home. The route took me across a small municipal park. It was a sad and grimy off-green place; as if all leaves were dulled by the city's polluted air, the paths worn stone and cold. Trees that meant nothing. It was a short cut through my inner self, through the saddened entrails. Often I would sit on one of the park benches, made, I used to suppose, for the old and the defeated, and stare. And do my best not to think. But still the words used to come into my mind: this is the end of my life. None of the spirit in me, nothing of what I did best or loved, was able to grow. I painted in despair; went out some weekends to the Derbyshire countryside I knew; had some friends, a neighbour, a few people I could do things with, but there was nothing that I wanted to do that I did do. My passion for and elaborate knowledge of birds had disappeared under the inner wreckage. My love of fishing was a distant memory – can a child already have memories that feel distant? Yes. That's how it was. I was just eighteen.

I went to the accountants' office Mondays to Fridays, nine to five, and on alternate Saturdays nine to one. Pay rolls and accounts, column after column of pounds, shillings and pence. So we sat and went through one page after another, all day, every day. A break in this endless task would come in the form of checking totals out loud, with all the excitement of human exchange: 'Forty-eight pounds, thirteen shillings, nine pence.' 'Right.' 'One hundred and seventy-two pounds, eight shillings, four pence halfpenny.' 'Right, but drop the halfpenny.' We wore our suits, sat in two medium-sized spaces, called each other by our surnames, and went out for lunch in separate directions. Perhaps there was more to the hours spent there, but whatever I did or thought when there in that office, other than adding up and calling out confirmation of some number at the foot of a page of numbers, sank away into quagmires of dismay. I did become very good at arithmetic – my highest achievement that autumn of 1961 was being able to add the pounds, shillings and pence as a single line.

The long autumn turned into winter. Some evenings when I got home I was speechless with a kind of hopeless anger, or angry hopelessness. I began to feel a kind of weakness in the body, limbs that had lost their force, that could not take my weight, and my mind blacked out, not so much with grim thoughts as with the grimness of too few thoughts. Bit by bit, day by day, the meaning seeped out of life; there were palliatives, avoidance of the bleakness, but there seemed no way to find meaning, no way to find a reason for enduring much more of this. No one to talk to, nowhere to turn where I could begin to speak of my unhappiness.

My sense of having no future was so complete that it obscured the possibility of there being a present. Without quite finding the decision – I have no memory of thoughts that took the steps of a decision – it occurred to me that I could kill myself. A year before, I had been given a shotgun. So the obvious way for me to do it was with this gun. I kept it in its leather case on the floor of my attic room.

In my memory I am in that attic bedroom sometime after going up to bed; there is the darkness of night and the darkness of hopelessness. I sit on the bed feeling there is no way to get out of this state of mind. Not thoughts so much as a grey and empty sadness. It comes back to me now as I write this. No concern for others, no image of what it would mean to them, no idea of writing a note, of sending a message to explain or achieve understanding, no vision of the mess that would be made – be it the mess that comes from shotgun wounds or the mess of a family that would have to deal with it all. There was no one to send a note to. No interest in communicating with anyone. Nothing, that is, except this statement: the explosion of a shotgun cartridge signalling that I had reached the end of the bleak road that I was on. This, after all, is the state of mind in which death makes itself welcome, so I did not turn in any way to others. It is a disconnect that strikes me now, as the centre of the memory. Perhaps I am not able to bring to mind, sixty years later, what that mind was. Yet much of that late evening is vivid to me still – I see myself as I sat on the bed, the darkness, a bedside light, the furniture, the window out onto the roof. But there are no thoughts. Something behind or beyond thought: a wordless realisation and its simple resolution. An emptiness that was the measure of the emptiness of life. A sense that the unbearableness of it all could be dealt with – by taking the gun, loading it, and shooting myself in the head. Obliterating the mind that had so little way of helping itself. The flow from that time into this, from the state of mind then to the flow of words now, is surprising for its force and its clarity. I had grown up with so much silence, and with the shadow of death cast from within this silence.

There is a difference, of course, between the things never spoken, the stories kept secret, and the memories that are for the first time recovered. Yet these two areas of unspoken mind are not so easy to separate. The zone where thoughts have blurred edges and uncertain detail, where words have never been used to take away the secrecy and remove some of the inner mystery, is where both recovered memory and unshared secrets lie. And so it was with the moment when I picked up the shotgun, loaded one of its chambers with a number five shot cartridge, and pointed it at my head. The boy sitting on a bed in the attic, bending forward, slumped but holding the gun around the trigger guard, leaning the barrel up towards his forehead. The length of it means he has to reach out and keep his head up for all that the shoulders are bent. I see myself there very still for a moment, a pause. The outside is firm, held as if in a photograph; the inside is dissolved, absent. I cannot remember the state of mind, a holding of its breath, a waiting for the event that is to happen. Nor do I have a memory of pulling the trigger, though I must have done, for the gun misfired.

Emerging from the blur of feelings, I had to focus on the practical. Something was wrong with the firing mechanism. I opened the breach of the gun and saw the firing pins sticking through, as they do after they have been released by the trigger into the head of the cartridge. They must have been faulty when I put the gun together. I spent some time checking what had happened and attempting to fix it. I realised that I did not know how, and said to myself that I could go the next day to see a gamekeeper I knew and have him sort out the problem.

And then I would be able to . . . to what? Sit again on the bed and shoot myself? I think that is what I thought, but I also am aware of a kind of flowing of air through my mind, a realisation, perhaps, that the crisis had passed and that there was no firm resolve to have another go. To be back in a position to have a go, maybe. I do not know if I asked myself what I intended to do once the gun was mended. But I did go the next day to visit my gamekeeper friend, driving the hour or so to his cottage, and showed him the problem with the firing pins. He fixed it without much difficulty and explained how I could sort it out the next time this happened – it was easy to get the firing pins back into the right position.

I never again sat on the side of that or any other bed and considered shooting myself. That feeling of utter hopelessness did not return, or not in that complete and unmanageable form. The darkness within me became something more familiar, less terrifying, less a source of self-pity and more a part of being a person – with a place, in my view, of what we all have to put up with at times. Difficulties can have some other facet, some origin that lies elsewhere. So crises, or my reaction to crises, seemed to be an echo or mysterious sound wave from a part of myself to which I had very little access. The problems I found myself thinking about were taking me to obscure and complex memories, to feelings of fearful intensity that came both from nowhere and also from the very heart of me.

A fragile shell had grown, a slight shield against the events and decisions that shaped the time leading up to my being an accountant's clerk; some protection from the mismatch between all that this boy was supposed to be and become, expecting it even of himself, and failing. History and bewildering choices make for the fragile shell. Once this flow of circumstances, this structure of life, has taken shape, it does not take much for the shell to crack.

I buried the events, the despairing night in the attic, the firing, or misfiring, of the shotgun. Somewhere between avoided and forgotten. It would be several decades, and a different encounter with suicide, before it all would come back into my thoughts.

There came to be a surprising escape, roads that did lead to elsewhere, to another kind of living in the world, or another way of being within history. I received an offer of a place to study Philosophy, Politics and Economics at Trinity College, Oxford. Then came research scholarships, a job teaching philosophy and then the discovery of anthropology. A life of journeys in search of meaning. Going to the margins to discover what lies at the centre.

ENGLAND

German words jump into my mind: *Was haben Sie getan?* What have they done? Or does it mean, rather: What did they do? Or is you, whom I respect, the singular *'Sie'*? Or you, the many of you? *Aber was haben Sie getan?* But what have they or you or both or all of you done? A song, a lament, from somewhere in history, from somewhere in the past.

———————

I am sitting on the floor, in front of the fireplace, watching the television. My mother is in the kitchen, two doors and a short hallway away. Sunlight is pouring into the room. It must be summer. Then the images begin, on the screen. There are rows of bunks in a long shack, and people lying there who are alive but too weak to do more than raise a head or sit, living skeletons, on a bench. Then people looking at the camera, in rags, starved. Heads that are skulls; eyes that are staring and glazed. Some soldiers are bringing them a lorry-load of food. They are handing out what looks like apples. Thin, feeble hands reach out to take one and begin to eat. It looks to me as if they are not strong enough, not quite alive enough, to eat. Then there is a pile of dead bodies, and soldiers carrying corpses to add to the pile. The dead and the dying. I understand that the soldiers have released prisoners, are saving lives, and helping to bury the dead. The dead, the dying; corpses;

starved humans who stare out at me from that screen. Heads that are skulls; living skeletons.

It is something so terrible, so agonised, that panic rises within me. I see it now, the sun in the room, the television in the corner, the death camp being liberated. I see it over and over, and feel it as, I think, I felt it then. A loop of images that is too terrible to turn away from. Replaying in the core of me: as I write this now I feel a sickness and fixity of horror that I must have felt then, a rising of fluid in the throat and my eyes flinching. Closing them on what I saw then. Or closing them now, better to be able to re-enter the horror.

I watched, then leaped to my feet. I stood for a moment, then turned and ran to the door, along the hall, into the kitchen, to find someone, to be away from those images, that place being shown on the television. And I had this thought in my head – I hear it now, shouting to me from back then, as clear as a thought can be for a child: that is me, there, starving and dying and dead. Those are my eyes staring out of the horror; my hand that reaches for an apple with not even the strength to seize it. That is me thrown on a pile of corpses, liberated in my rags by the soldiers in their uniforms. Me being killed.

My mother was there in the kitchen and must have done her best to cope with me, the distraught child, and with what he had seen on the screen. But the memory ends before there are any words of comfort or explanation. Perhaps I had already learned that this shock and grief could not be eased by my mother; or that even if she took me into her arms there would not be the comfort of words that were needed. That moment breaks through that which is forgotten or was never said.

I was nine years old.

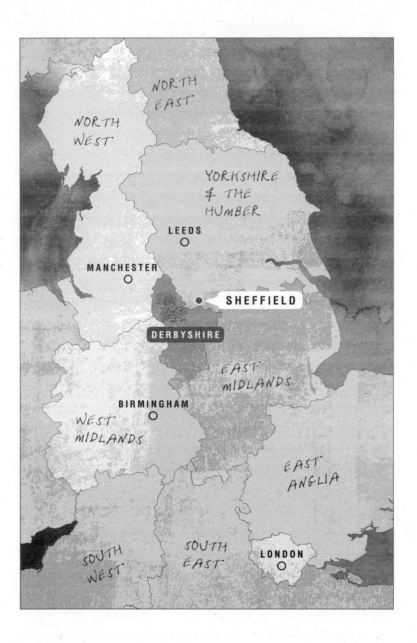

NORTH EAST

NORTH WEST

YORKSHIRE & THE HUMBER

LEEDS

MANCHESTER

SHEFFIELD

DERBYSHIRE

EAST MIDLANDS

BIRMINGHAM

WEST MIDLANDS

EAST ANGLIA

SOUTH WEST

SOUTH EAST

LONDON

From time to time, on a Sunday afternoon, at the bottom of the drive up to our quiet home at the fringes of a Sheffield suburb, close to the Derbyshire hills, deep in England, a strange figure would appear. A man in a dark overcoat, an old-fashioned hat, a nervous manner. On foot, appearing to have walked a long way, seeming to be lost, searching for the right house. It would be someone who had found our address through the local Jewish or Zionist network. Always a youngish man. He would come to the door, ring the bell, be let into the room my family called the lounge. He would sit there without taking off his coat or hat. He would want to speak to my father. He had timed the visit in the hope of finding him at home. There would be a long explanation that I could not understand, but to do with needing to get to, or get back to, Israel. A need for money to pay for the fare, or a request for a contribution to some Zionist fund. I could see that my father was embarrassed. He would listen, nodding and saying very little, then write a cheque.

For all that they were young, these disturbing men, in their long coats and unfamiliar hats, looked worn out, dilapidated – not like our usual visitors, not clean and neat. Their appearance caused unease, seemed designed to cause unease. Strangers came into our house who did not belong there, and yet had some claim on us. As if they embodied a reproach, or carried a memory that was best forgotten; or some slight breaking down of the family defences, an exposure to aliens. These uneasy visitors were representatives of orthodox Judaism, or the real Zionist. They should not be sitting there, in our chairs. Yet ours was a Jewish and Zionist house. The embarrassment of my father may have been his awareness of contradictions, or his being found out in a home that was more secular than it should have been, and more ambivalent about Zionism than it would admit to.

Cheder is Hebrew for 'room', and has long been used to mean the classroom where Jewish children learn the language, law and customs of Judaism and prepare for bar mitzvah. *Bar* is an Aramaic and Hebrew word with a double meaning: it is the word for 'son', but in rabbinical teachings it is deemed also to mean 'subject to'; *mitzvah* means law or commandment as well as the good deeds performed by following them. So my brother and I went to the *cheder* – every Sunday morning, Saturdays after the synagogue service and on Wednesday evenings after school – to be prepared to be subjected to the commandments and to absorb what it means to be good.

We learned to read and write Hebrew, listened to the volunteers from the Sheffield Jewish community who gave their time as amateur teachers, and to lectures on the Talmud from the community's rabbi. As we came close to bar mitzvah we also learned to sing, or intone, passages from the Torah, following the tiny symbols – the cantillations, the *ta-amim* – above and below the lines of Hebrew that signalled melodic intonations. Each of the incantation symbols had a name that we had to sing out with its proper up and down of voice – *mahpa-ach* (with the *a-ach* going down and then up in two short lurches), *pahst-ta'a* (the *ta'a* going up and then down). Generation after generation of Jewish children had been taken through these exercises.

To learn the language, and to be able to intone a passage of Hebrew, was an entry into a secret code. I had the worst possible singing voice, was banned from all choirs at school, teased for tunelessness at home, but intoning in the wavering, uncertain manner of a synagogue cantor gave me pleasure. The rest of the classes did not. They were boring and often took place when I was tired and longed to be at home. I would stare out of the windows and daydream. My brother would do all he could to make sure we arrived late.

These lessons my brother and I had to endure in the run-up to our bar mitzvahs were more than instructions in Judaism. They were shaped by the single-minded optimism of post-war Zionism. We were shown pictures of the new Israel, told about the making of orange groves where there had been nothing but arid desert, and told that life in Israel was honest, hard-working, healthy. We were encouraged to join a Zionist equivalent of the Boy Scouts, where boys and girls learned skills and attitudes that would prepare them for emigration to the promised land. But in our family there was a tentative quality about this part of Zionism: to know about Israel, to care about it, to want to visit – we were encouraged in all of these. As small children we were given to understand that *Eretz Yisrael*, the land of Israel, was a great achievement, a triumph. Yet the idea that we might go and live there was alarming to parents like mine, who were all the time concerned that we assimilate and thrive in England. It was no part of what I as a child imagined as adventure. Better to join the ordinary Boy Scouts than get caught up in that Zionist version.

The achievement in our family was the home that had been created in Sheffield, the north of England; to leave this for an alternative home in Israel would be a betrayal of that achievement, a leaping into something between a Bible story and a state of nature. The appeal of Israel for those who had become steeped in

the Zionist vision of a return to an ancestral home, set up a sharing of the ownership of land, celebrated manual over intellectual
labour, repudiated the traditional Jewish skills and professions,
rejected the whole complex of European high culture – all this
caused unease to my kind of family. There was also within the
Zionism of the 1940s a readiness to take up arms. We might
be Zionists, keen supporters of the new Jewish nation-state, but
in our family the children's lives were shaped by old-fashioned
European ideals – of culture and civilisation, acceptance of whatever might be deemed to be the English way of life; not a return
to some elemental form of farming or the military.

To imply that the home in the suburbs of Sheffield was not,
after all, safe and secure, and all that we needed, was to undermine
the family project. We did not locate the story of Israel in the
events of the war. No mention was made of the camps, the losses,
the destruction of European Jews. These reasons for needing to get
to Israel or wanting to fortify that new nation-state were not given
to us. Neither at home nor in the *cheder* were there any accounts,
or lessons, that could be called modern history. The law came from
God; the story was rooted in the Old Testament. We sang our passages from the Torah with minimal understanding of the Hebrew
words and no sense at all that this was to sing out in survival.

———

Packed in old boxes and stuck in pre-war albums there are many
photographs of my mother as a plump baby, a pretty toddler, a
girl, an elegant young woman. As a teenager she holds herself in
front of the camera with great assurance, aware of her good looks
and, it seemed, happy to be photographed. In those old black and

white prints she is sultry and dark-skinned, but this may in part be the quality of the images, and in part a result of photographs being taken on holidays in the sun. She is Viennese, intense, beautiful and, she would tell us, much occupied with boyfriends. She did well at school; was educated into the Viennese haute-bourgeois sophistications; she was taken to the opera; she could skate and ski; she had learned English and some French and wrote well; she wanted to study medicine, to become a doctor. The war changed all that: she escaped Vienna, just, and found herself in England, working as a nurse in a Sheffield hospital – where, in a few weeks, she met and fell in love with a doctor, my father, and remained in Sheffield for the rest of her life.

––––––––

My father was small and with the Eastern European looks associated with the *shtetl* – very dark hair, strong features, intense brown eyes. His first names were Hyman Pinchas. His father was Jona and his mother was Dora. He had an older sister, Sarah, and a younger brother, Morris. He went to a Sheffield grammar school and from there to Sheffield University. My mother often told us with a retrospective but rather wistful pride that he was offered a scholarship to study mathematics at Cambridge, and he told me that he had wanted to go and work in India. He spoke only English, having learned no more than scraps of Yiddish, yet had been expected to centre his whole life in the Jewish home and Jewish community. He had been able to take part in life that was not limited to the synagogue: he played both football and cricket for his school, and was enthusiastic enough about theatre, especially Shakespeare, to become secretary of the school drama society and was prompter in school plays. He was an enthusiastic support-er of Sheffield Wednesday football team and the Yorkshire cricket club. He must have longed for a life that could take him far from his home in Sheffield.

But his parents were adamant: mathematics was not a suitable subject for a Jewish boy. He should go to Sheffield University and become a dentist. He did as was demanded, and was bored and frustrated by dentistry. So he turned to medicine. He did not leave his Jewish home, did not begin to live a life that was his own, until he met my mother and, with her, on the strength of her, depend-ing on her stories, they set up home together. He was thirty-three, she was nineteen.

My mother told us many times that when her beloved Hyman proposed to her, her answer was that she could not marry because she had to take care of her mother. So Hyman declared that her mother must live with them when they married. Perhaps this was thought to be a temporary arrangement, a dealing with the crisis of her displacement and impoverishment. The war in Europe was under way, and all could see that Britain would soon be caught in this war. So the mother-in-law was part of the household from its start. And remained a part until she fell down dead in the kitchen twenty-eight years later.

We called her Oma – 'Grandma' in German (and, I was later to discover, almost the exact same word in Afrikaans). I had no sense of it being from a foreign language, though; it seemed to be a word that belonged in the family, coming from its private realities. In fact, Oma was very much a woman from elsewhere, or from a Europe that in those days seemed a long way removed and a life that was exotic to the point of being fantastical. She was small, a little stooped, but blazed with energy – she raged about politics, cooked in fury in defiance of blindness. Her features were strong – sharply defined chin, high forehead, distinct cheekbones. Her hair was thick and there was an air of diminished elegance about her. Her eyes and expression were keen, determined – she peered with a ferocious will to see, defying and fighting against the blurred darkness. In our front room the television stood on the right-hand side of the fireplace, a curved screen built into its wooden cabinet. An armchair was placed very close, where Oma could sit: her near-blindness meant she had to peer into the screen from a few inches, angled so as not to block others' view, and forever causing shouts of dismay: 'We can't see! We can't see!'

This struggle to see and fury at not being able to see came to represent Oma's character, an effort of her mind as well as her eyes. She was a woman of strong opinions and a good deal of education; civilised in an old meaning of this term, or with a need for civilisation – knowledge of the arts, appreciation of great music, speaking five languages, insisting upon and noticing good manners. Along with this there was a conservatism and an unselfconscious snobbery which came from another era, and which led her to insist that British imperial achievements were remarkable and a force for good, whereas England, with its parochial philistinism, was grim.

Yet it was in this England that she was marooned. She used to tell me that she had always thought of England as a rock out in the Atlantic. She could never have imagined having a home there. Once Europe was falling to the Nazis, she decided to leave altogether: they – she and my mother – would go to India. She had bought the tickets, shipped some of her things, had planned for my mother to do medicine at Bombay University . . . But she was prevented from making this complete escape by her daughter falling in love with a Sheffield doctor and refusing to continue with the escape plan. Unable to see, all her resources gone, the Soviet government having seized her husband's family's estates in Poland and the Ukraine, the Nazis having taken all she had in Vienna, she was dependent on this daughter. This wayward, obstinate, love-sick daughter. Who was insisting on marrying a Jewish doctor in Sheffield. In England.

My mother was a remarkable and dedicated cook. There were Central European favourites prepared with the greatest care – wiener-schnitzel, borscht, goulasch, piroghi, and, best of all for us children, the cakes and pastries. Chocolate éclairs, home-made blackcurrant ice-cream, tarte au citron, meringues layered with lemon sauces and huge, multi-storey coffee-cream gâteaux. Then the English food: kippers for breakfast or roast beef and Yorkshire pudding for Sunday lunch. We understood that all our food was symbolic, some kind of metaphor, to do with memory, ideas of civilisation, or a defiance of the evil workings of history. What we ate, how we ate it, the plates we ate it off – tastes and meanings combined. Even the Yorkshire pudding: cooked in a separate, single tin and made in such a way as to cause it to rise so high that it reached the top of the oven – a triumph each time it appeared, an alpine range of perfection, scorch marks at the peaks to prove it. My mother did all she could to turn the most ordinary food into something spectacular, but to be a cook of English food at this level, to these heights, we were given to understand, you had to come from Vienna.

It was a belief in, a memory of, a celebration of a world that was lost, that had been taken and destroyed, but a heritage that lived on, that had to live on, in defiance of all else; or, if not in defiance, then with a willingness to incorporate all that was seeking to hide or replace it. To cook so well was her prevailing over everything, and yet the food was a reminder that she came from somewhere other. It affirmed Vienna, not Jewishness, an achievement of universal value, a matter of great pride, yet the full meaning of this cuisine was also buried in silence. She cooked to take pride in Vienna but, above all, as a part of being safe, as a contribution she made to our safety. It was to be herself within the sanctuary of Sheffield.

Those first years, as the Austrian wife of a Sheffield doctor, she must have sounded very foreign, though she did all she could to become as English as possible. For all that she did not shed the Viennese lilt to her voice, she was fluent in English. She prided herself on being able to do the *Times* crossword puzzle. Every afternoon she listened to *Mrs Dale's Diary* on 'the wireless'; every evening it was *The Archers*. She never sought to obscure our Jewish identity, and went at times to the synagogue, but she believed our future, like her safety, lay in being English.

Yet she was often angry. Sometimes she raged. Some of this was focused on the mother she never got away from, but the terrifying explosions of anger were directed at us children and, I think, most of all at me. Her need for order, her ideas of cleanliness or propriety, some sense of what was and was not good behaviour, would cause her to strike out at me – with threats, and sometimes with violence. I felt the shock of this: coming home from being out on some small adventure full of happiness and keen to tell some story of what I had been doing, and slamming into a wall of disapproval. I was too dirty, and had torn my shirt, or I knew not why. There would be a burst of complaint against me, a rough hauling off to the bathroom. Again and again that sense of failing to be the right sort of person, and fearing what this would mean. A looking for love; the shock of love becoming an attack on me.

Sometimes my brother and I were threatened with a horse whip that our mother claimed she had in a large clothes cupboard, ready for the purpose. This threat never came to anything, and I am not sure we ever quite believed that this whip existed – though our dread was real enough. But there were times when she would lose control, become some desperate person – her hands crashing into my face, slaps that were almost punches. I don't know how often this happened, and I must have been very small. It was enough to instil in me a primitive fear of her that remained long after the apparent innocence and the naive inarticulacy of childhood had passed: for many years a horror of being touched by her, even of her standing near me.

My mother was fierce, passionate about her family and yet had so much difficulty expressing love for her children. Her eruptive anger, her tense and complicated internal life, meant that I was wary of her from a very young age. I see now that the deaths of so many of her relatives must have tormented and haunted her, and she was having children, in 1940 and 1943, at just the time when her family was being dispossessed and murdered. Her silence about the deaths may have been an essential way for her to survive, and yet an added torment for her. I have to suppose that the shadows of death and loss were a form of continuous trauma, making any flow of love close to impossible; or that only the love of her husband, and her husband's love for her, were the protection she could turn to and depend on. It was the only form of love she could allow in herself.

My brother and I grew up in the 1940s and '50s, so we were children at a time when ideals of middle-class life conspired to nurture a lack of love, or lack of its expression. Of course, we could not conceptualise love, however much we longed for it, and, at times, at night, we sensed that there was something that we need-ed but could not have. Our parents perhaps defied this, with and within the passion of their marriage; they had not been given the words, or any idea of the need for words, with which to attack and open up their 'lonely fortress', neither by the society in which they lived, nor by any possibility of becoming emotionally articulate. History, class, society, the war, themselves. The past was too much arraigned against them, preventing them from giving their chil-dren the kind of love in which we could find ourselves and from which we might be able to learn to love others.

In the background of my mother's new home and my grand-mother's new life on the cold Atlantic rock, on the other side of the English Channel, in the places they had once thought of as home, unspeakable horror was unfolding. This must have been omnipresent for them. And much of what defined her – the Austrian refugee speaking German, living in a new landscape, the young wife whom everybody saw as exotic and many criti-cised as not good enough or not Jewish enough or just not right for the Sheffield doctor she had married – was not even a day's slow travel away, where a war was raging.

Yet my mother told us only scraps and glimpses of her history, just fragments of stories. My brother, three years older, and I grew up within a profound silence. We were told nothing about the events that in so many ways had defined us, given birth to us. At least, we were taught nothing about these events by parents or at school. The silence in our home about the horrors of the war was matched by a public silence.

At no time, in not a single lesson, as no part of any classroom conversation or talk given to the school, did I hear about the Holocaust. There were talks which included recollections of being in the armed forces in the Second World War, a teaching of German as a foreign language, a reading and long discussions of Jean Anouilh's *Pauvre Bitos*, a play about those who had collaborated with the Nazis – all this managed to take place without a reference to, still less an account of, the death camps. Even in the last year of school, when the teaching might have claimed to be broad and imaginative, aiming to prepare the more academic boys for entrance exams to Oxford and Cambridge, the war remained as something rather glorious. It was talked about, and known, if that is not too generous a word, as a great battle between two impressive armies. Heroism on both sides; a fine victory for our boys, for Great Britain.

We got our images of modern history from a weekly delivery of *Eagle*, one of the most popular comics of the 1950s and '60s. In its pages we met German soldiers who were full of fighting spirit and forever shouting '*Donner und Blitzen*', and the rather better-looking British lads who always prevailed in the heat of honourable battle. Well, not quite so honourable always, on the German side. They did behave badly towards those British officers and men in prisons; true heroes were planning and at times executing magnificent escapes. As for mass murder, rounding up of whole communities, trains flowing to the death camps; as for the killing of the Jews, gypsies, homosexuals and the disabled – of this not a word.

The silence in our home was thus part of a much wider and greater silence. Our childhood was to be kept innocent, and the children protected from any such horror – this was how it would have been felt or expressed in our family. My mother needed to make her life here, in the north of England, in a suburban house, in the English language. She needed to succeed in this move, absorb the new landscapes and attitudes and preoccupations of her new home, to make it a home, so she needed to forget. Or to know what was happening over there in the arenas of murder only in a very private internal zone. Some of this knowledge reached her at the end of the war and in the first years of peace, when we children were already able to talk and hear and understand. So she had the self-appointed task of keeping from us the news of another death, another atrocity, the details of yet more losses, as they emerged from the ruins of the camps or from the lists of victims put together by the Red Cross.

I do not know if she scoured the lists, searching for the names of relatives, friends, neighbours. I think not. There was a silence that must have reached so deep into her: the absence of the people she had known as a child, the disappearance of the world in which she had lived, gone to school, made friends, had holidays, first been in love . . . Not a word from anyone there, and no chance to go again to those altered places. The pain of this is hard to imagine, especially as she would not share it, keeping it away from everyone, even from her husband. She had moved, to safety; she had shut out the history, silenced its devastating messages, and cut herself off from herself in order to protect us all. The chatter of everyday life, the home, even with its arguments and contradictions, everything depended on silence. In each domain, family life and global *realpolitik*, the need to move on, to build a new world, was fused with complex reasons for at least the appearance of amnesia. So she could not talk to us about anything.

But my grandmother, my Oma, whispered to me: when I was in bed and she came to say goodnight, sharing a few words at the end of the day, or sometimes when we were alone together in the house. Then, in a taut and hushed voice, letting me know that this was something between the two of us, our secret, in defiance of the others, she told me that there were things I must know, even though I would not understand them. Things to do with being a Jew. Even though she had never thought of herself as a Jew, she said, or had never thought Jewishness mattered. She only knew a smattering of Hebrew, and had not created rituals in her own home, had not been a member of a synagogue. But it did matter. This was what she needed to whisper to me, to share with me, to plant in me: it mattered far more than she had ever thought. You could never escape, she said, and you should not try to escape.

She whispered this to me. So this was a secret? No, not this, since we all could know and all must know that to be a Jew was part of the family we were in. It was something else. She had learned this because of what had happened. Because of the Germans, because of Hitler. Terrible things had been done – she would not speak of them, they happened in the war. But these terrible things meant that no one would ever forget that you were a Jew. Many had been killed because of this Jewishness.

One woman, a survivor friend Oma had met in Sheffield, came to visit, and Oma pointed to the row of little bluish numbers on her friend's wrist. Look at those numbers, she would whisper, they tell you that you can't forget, that they won't let you forget. That voice in my ear, those words about some unspecified disaster, that pointing out of the numbers: I remember the feeling of it as much as her voice, her there sitting beside me when I was sleeping in a bed in the converted attic. I do not know how old I was when the whispering began, four or five perhaps. And she told me more some years later, when I was seven or eight. How much between those times? Enough to reach far into me.

This whispering may have been intended as a refusal of concealment. But to whisper a secret is to point to the unspoken, to make evident the large, infinite zone beyond the hearing, to the place where the real and smothering silence stretched out far and wide. I was given knowledge that I could not know about. It became an elusive, obscure part of me. Something between fact and sensation. These people called Nazis, Hitler, Germans – they did terrible things to people like me. So I was terrified of what had happened, of what could happen, of something out there that was unfathomable, that was so dreadful that my Oma would whisper it to me; troubled and frightening feelings were seeded within me, rooting in obscure and dark corners. I knew there was something I did not know, or did know some fragments of, enough to know that there was more to know, and to understand that this was something no one else would tell me. I had suffered no pain, had lost no one, yet I was being told, in these intense whispers, that there was pain everywhere for people like me, and losses beyond counting. How could I have grasped the murmured facts or some puzzling thoughts about things a child would not have understood? To grasp what was being told I would have had to know it all already.

Yet there was some way in which that small child I once was knew everything. The world leaks its truths as much as Oma leaked hers – in the darkness of the night, at the borders of sleep, in the depths of unconsciousness – and the child senses what is real. Even if the real has to be buried beyond reach, or spoken of, released into everyday life, as something else, perhaps something that is not real; even if the things a child is told are a mix of facts and evasions, or untruths, the real is there as a hidden challenge, or a deep source of bewilderment – as the child attempts to match what it knows to what it is told.

———————

A first and early escape from this bewilderment lay just across the road. Our house was on a long hill, going from the city, at the bottom, to wide-open moorland at the top. Right opposite our house, a gate opened onto a churchyard, leading into a spread of graves, tombs, pathways, bushes, brambles. Low walls divided one level of graves from the next. This was the world that lay between us, at one side, and the main road, with its line of shops, on the other. A world of trees, thickets, hedgerows and meandering paths – some of it with raked gravel and neat arrangements of flowers on the graves, and some of it wild and tangled with neglect. The distance across this terrain, so vast in my memory, with its hints of wilderness, and the ordering of the dead, must have been less than half a mile's walk.

One day on a journey across the cemetery to the shops, when I must have been no more than five years old, I found a song thrush nest in a small bush by the side of a steep path, between a railing and a grave. Three eggs so blue they gleamed, with tiny splashes of black dots, in a clay white cup. I took one of the eggs: such an amazing discovery could not be left untouched. The nest cast its spell. From then on, my search for more such nests and their eggs took me ever deeper into the least tended, most overgrown and forgotten parts of the cemetery. There is the slimmest divide in my mind between that first, sparkling blue thrush egg and the climbing, clambering, searching that led to so many more. The moment of first discovery, the gateway into the graves and adventures, became a search for all the nests and eggs that could be found. Exploration of the churchyard, the discovery of its birds, began to merge with a childish scholarship that reached far, far beyond that one place.

Many song thrushes and blackbirds, as well as greenfinch, chaffinch, bullfinch and linnet; mistle thrush, hedge sparrow, wren, robin and, once, a willow warbler. Even a spotted flycatcher. I found these nests in the churchyard, and then in any other patch of suburban hedge or bushes I happened to pass by. Clambering, crawling, peering, hoping to find another cluster of eggs, warm in their nest, discovering and learning the differences, I came to life.

We went on Sundays for lunch at a rather grand but dilapidated hotel in a village in Derbyshire, very close to the immense grounds of Chatsworth House. It was only half an hour's drive from home, but it seemed to be another continent. Its gardens were large and thick with flowers – I was astonished by towering lupins and gleaming peonies. There was a stream running along the side of this garden, another world of birds, with species that were exotic to me: grey wagtails, a flash of a kingfisher, a first glimpse of a dipper. Behind Chatsworth House there rose a hillside of dense rhododendrons. We would walk through the park and gardens and up the slopes, our family on its sedate Sunday afternoon outing: along the paths that went back and forth across and up that forest of a hillside. I would dive off into the rhododendrons, searching high and low, through the bushes, into the undergrowth and up into the trees. At the highest point of the walk, far above the house, was a lake; mallards and little grebes nested there. In my memory it is always spring: birdsong, and the finding of eggs.

A woman who must have been the manager of the hotel where we had our Sunday lunches had noticed this small boy who was forever in search of birds. We did not know her and yet, out of the magical nowhere that is the whole universe beyond the child, one Sunday lunchtime she appeared with a large, black book. It was a worn copy of *British Birds* by Kirkman and Jourdain. She gave it to me. It was a miracle: to have this book, in which every species ever to be found in Britain was described and depicted – its colour plates shone, alive to me as an image could be. All the important facts about every bird: what it ate, its song and, most thrilling and miraculous of all, detailed accounts of nests and eggs – what the nest was made of; how many eggs were laid; the most eggs ever found, and the fewest; the average size; how long each species needed to hatch; then how long before the chick would fledge. And there, as the final, beautiful section of this great work: pages and pages of eggs, to exact scale and showing the range of all the colour forms that had ever been seen. Everything about everything that I wanted to know.

I still have that book, very battered and with untidy, boyhood marks through the index, alongside species after species, to show that I had found its nest. It was with me all through childhood. These were the post-war years; people like us did not travel more than very short distances from home. All those nests and eggs could be found only in those pages at the back of the book. So I journeyed in my imagination as far as the Scottish Highlands to find the sea eagle or the capercaillie, and to the South Downs to come across a hoopoe or a wryneck. I looked at their nests and collected their eggs from the pictures and descriptions on those pages of a perfect book.

Again and again I handed my copy of *British Birds* to my mother or grandmother and insisted that they open it at random, tell me the name of the bird on the page in front of them, and I would declare, without a flicker of hesitation, where that bird nested, what it made its nest from, how many eggs it laid and what colour they were. Jackdaw – a hole in a tree; made out of sticks, lined with grasses; 4–7 eggs, rarely 3 or 8; green background covered with dark blotches. Golden eagle – on a cliff face or high in a tree; a great pile of sticks; 2–3, rarely 1; pale background covered with reddish or black spots and streaks. Long-tailed tit – in a bush or hedge; a round ball of moss and lichens lined with hundreds of feathers; 10–15 eggs, sometimes even more; white with very small, pale spots. On and on I would go, further and further into this mass of detail, this specialised knowledge, into knowledge itself, into territories and landscapes and images that were mine and yet were so much from elsewhere.

My grandmother always urged me on. To know such things, to know, is to . . . is to . . . what? Be right? Make a world that I could name? Use labels to discover a way of having control? Defy the incomprehensible? Defy silences? Live as one should? Escape? And if escape, escape from where? Sheffield? England? The whispered facts and thoughts that conjured up disaster and loss and suffering? Those terrible images on the television one summer afternoon? Perhaps all I understood then was that in knowledge I could find a special and essential happiness.

In the summer of 1953 we went to stay in a house on the banks of the Thames for a month. I dug for worms, gathered them in a tin can, and set out to explore the river at the bottom of the garden. The water was deep and slow-moving, and a bit faster out in the middle. Easy fishing.

I found a rod, reel, a packet of hooks, dug for worms, and spent much of every day on that bank, casting out baits, sitting and watching a float tied into the line a few feet above hook and worm. The float would drift in the current, then stop, tremble, duck a little into the water and, if a fish was sure that this was real food, would dive, pulled down below the surface. I learned to give the rod a quick tug, just as the float dived. I caught my first perch, with leathery striped sides and spiked dorsal fin, and my first roach, an elegant mix of large dorsal fin, silver sides and orange fins. If I fished very deep, I caught gudgeon, dark and densely patterned with huge eyes and many fins. Once I almost hooked a pike: it seized a fish I was winding in, tugging it back down towards the reeds, letting go as I lifted predator and its victim towards the surface.

There were birds, of course. Kestrels dropping down on their prey right across the river from the garden bank where I fished; kingfishers hurtling in a gleam of blue along the surface in front of me; stock doves, sand martins and a heron that came to the garden pond in search of goldfish. But my eyes were for much of the time fixed on the river, focused on the float that gave such exciting hints of what was happening below, down there near the bottom of the river, where my bait was dangling and inviting the fish to be caught.

The year after the summer of fishing on the bank of the Thames I made friends with a boy at school called Alex. He told me that he did lots of fishing, with his father, and that in the spring I must come with them. So that April, in 1954, I was invited to come for a Sunday family picnic by the River Manifold, a small stream that winds through south-west Derbyshire, about an hour's drive from our house in Sheffield. Alex's father was a fly-fisherman, and he gave me my first lessons in casting weightless imitation insects out onto the surface of the river. Among the treats of the day was a picnic – with salmon and cucumber sandwiches, of which I ate a very large number.

Except that on the way home, twisting and turning along the Derbyshire roads, packed tight into the back of the car – Alex's mother sat in the front, while we were squashed in the back with his sister and grandmother – I was overcome with carsickness. This was an old problem of mine. Overcome also with shyness, I struggled to defy that which could not be defied for long: I held it in. Too late I cried out, 'I think I am going to be sick.' Too late, because the sick was on its way out right behind the words. I clamped my hand to my mouth. The pressure from within was great. Vomit sprayed between my fingers. We were going round a long bend – the trees and wall close to the side of the road, nowhere to stop. I turned to the open window, hoping that this disaster could be made less terrible by pouring out through it, though also onto it. At last the car stopped, and I climbed out, drenched in sick, humiliated to the limits of humiliation. I was helped out of my sodden clothes, wrapped in a blanket, and driven home.

Alex's family forgave my carsickness, though a reek of it must have reminded them of that picnic for a long time. They invited me to their house, far on the other side of the city, close to industrial rather than suburban landscapes. Sunday lunch. We sat at the table – Alex, his sister, his father and his grandmother. Alex's mother brought in a plate piled with Yorkshire pudding – flat and large pieces – and a jug of gravy. Did I like Yorkshire pudding? Yes, I said, very much, though I had never seen it in this form, looking like dark-coloured, wide and thick pancakes – so unlike the ones my grandmother prided herself on, which rose out of a baking tin with high crisped sides. And I had never been offered it as a course on its own. For us, it was on the side of roast beef, with potatoes and vegetables. I supposed that this was to be our lunch: the pile of puddings was high. But it tasted good, and all the better for the thick gravy – also new to me. So I determined to make the best of this strange but delicious meal. I ate a plateful, and accepted a second and then a third helping. I am sure I said that I had never had such good Yorkshire pudding, though I did feel a little concerned that this was all we would get. Well, I supposed there would be some kind of dessert. Then, plates cleared, I was astounded to see a large joint of beef appear, dishes of potatoes, vegetables – Sunday lunch. I struggled to manage. And then apple pie with cheese, and I heard the Yorkshire adage for the first time: 'Apple pie without the cheese is like the kiss without the squeeze.'

It was my first day ever deep inside the society that was England.

My father was most alive to us, most present, on Seder nights – the ritual Passover dinner at which Jewish families gather to tell the Bible story of the escape from slavery in Egypt. Passover as the celebration of freedom. My mother and grandmother prepared all the food: bitter herbs to evoke the suffering, lamb and unleavened bread to remind us of the last dinner and the need for haste – all leading to escape.

I was the youngest at the dinner, so I had to ask the Four Questions, for my father to answer them. What is the meaning of these things we eat, these things we do? My father read and sang the reply. Prayers and stories, chapter by chapter of the Haggadah, the book that appeared each year with copies for children full of brightly coloured pictures.

My father held this book of hope and from his place at the head of the table, glowing with happiness, at peace with us and with himself as on no other night of the year, he recited and sang his Jewishness, his identification, and all our identifications, with the slaves in Egypt, the appearance of Moses, the plagues sent by God, the opening of the Red Sea, the escape to a promised land. And shared with us his background, his feelings for the family, his story. On that one night we were Jewish without complications; my parents joined together as a family to define us through a set of stories, with their unquestioned meanings. My brother and I, yarmulkas perched on our heads, were joined in every part of it, absorbed for this one long night into our Jewish home. When the table was laid with a place for the possible arrival of the prophet Elijah and the door opened to allow in any Jewish stranger who might be out there in the street needing to join a Seder, my heart beat loud and for a few moments I held my breath, in awe, sure that this year the miracle would happen . . .

My father's sister Sally, her husband Issy and their daughter Elizabeth always joined us for the two nights of Seder. They were the only close relatives who often came to our house, yet they too maintained a troubling distance and silence. I would learn, many years later, that Sally and Issy did not much like my mother – seeing her as foreign, too assimilated, not the right person for my father to marry. So they were polite and distant, sharing important events, like the Seder, but not breaching the fortresses around us. Elizabeth was ten years older than me, a girl then young woman, with wonderful red hair. I was in silent awe of her, but she seemed to take no interest in any of us. She let it be known that she was very much her father's daughter, and determined that her socialist ideals would shape her life. In due course, as I was to find out for myself, this led her into the socialist wing of Zionism.

This was the full extent of the family in Sheffield that would gather together. My father's parents would not eat with us – our house was not kosher, my mother did not observe all the Jewish rules about food. But on Seder night we were as Jewish as we could be, and it was then that my father had his place in the family. His joy at this shines down through the decades. The feelings on a Seder night remind me that in some way I longed for what it revealed – the father in his place, my heritage that was both omni-present and confused.

———————

I had a conventional, elaborate, generous, terrifying bar mitzvah. Despite my limited ability to sing in tune, and stage fright that turned my insides to jelly, I poured out my solo to a crowded synagogue, and stumbled through a mess of a thank you speech to the hundreds of guests at the next day's reception in the Sheffield Grand Hotel. But a few years later, by the time I was fifteen, I no longer went to the synagogue on Saturdays or even for the great festivals. I did not join my father even on Yom Kippur. My parents continued to do the Seder night, which still held its magic, even for the determined atheist I had become. And I always asked that set of questions on Seder night, still took pleasure in reading

Hebrew, and followed my father as, with his soft and beautiful voice, he sang the blend of history, culture and family.

It had nothing much to do with belief in God. It was easy to translate these ideas, and the rituals that went along with them, into secular or symbolic terms, a delicious set of metaphors. The brutality of the tyrant; the drama of the escaping slaves; the shedding of tears and spilling of blood; the miraculous destruction of the tyrant's army in the waves of the Red Sea. These were moral and political truths, given force by religious ritual, but not dependent on belief. Perhaps I understood, even as a fifteen year old, that this was a ceremony about the human condition and society, not any particular religion, not even dependent on God. These were stories that underpinned unhappiness. And this unhappiness could be touched on, addressed, dealt with – at least in a flow of inchoate feeling – by a poignant tangling of history and myth, and a family sitting together at the dinner table, for at least this once a year, sharing who we were. The Chosen People were at first the Jews in Egypt, then, as time went by, all people who needed and longed for their liberation.

A PROMISED LAND

In March 1962 I went to Israel. The gap between the accountancy office and university; an escape from Sheffield; a journey to the land, *Eretz Yisrael*, that was held to be of such importance yet without shape; an idea rather than a real place. My cousin Elizabeth was living in Zikim, a Mapam kibbutz – with its socialist ideal of Zionism – at the border of the Gaza Strip. She had been there long enough to be a full member of the community, married and with two daughters. I set off to visit her, Zikim, socialism, the desert and Israel.

By train to Marseilles; a boat from Marseilles – a storm in the Mediterranean and a delay in Naples. A plane from Rome to Tel Aviv. The journey had taken more than a week, ending with a two-hour bus ride from Tel Aviv to Ashkelon and fifteen minutes in a taxi from Ashkelon to Zikim. Journeys within Israel were short and fast.

It was late afternoon. I walked from the kibbutz gates along a last bit of road to the kibbutz buildings. There were dense orange groves on one side, huge fields of grain on the other; the spring sun was hot but bearable. I smelt for the first time the intense wafts of orange blossom that filled the air. Perched on a fence wire was a European roller. I caught a glimpse of a hoopoe. This was farmland, orchards, the planting and transformation of the desert.

Elizabeth and her husband Arieh welcomed me. They were exhausted and distracted: that morning Elizabeth had given birth to her third child, another girl; it had happened in their kibbutz room. Arieh had delivered the baby; it was so fast they did not have time even to call the kibbutz midwife. It seemed auspicious that I should arrive on the same day as the baby. I sat for a while in their bed-sitting-room home, Elizabeth and baby on the bed, Arieh offering me a glass of cold water. Soon he hurried me off to see the two small houses where visitors stayed, at the other side of the kibbutz buildings, almost where the desert dunes began. He showed me the *chederochel*, the communal dining room, where I would be able to go, like everyone else who lived there, for all my meals, and the shop where I could get the things I needed. Not really a shop: some shelves with basic clothing, toothpaste, a few household items and cigarettes. There was no till or checkout; everyone wrote down what they had taken in a small notebook that lay on a table by the entrance – a record of needs met with no monetary payment. Arieh explained that my room, meals and supplies in the shop were free. In return, I would be expected to be able to work six ten-hour days per week. Someone would tell me what the jobs would be. He was keen to set out the principle that lay behind all he was showing me: from each according to their abilities, to each according to their needs. This was the ideal of the Mapam kibbutz.

———————

This was both a community and a farm. Agricultural and socialist – a determined opposition to the stereotypical Jewish realities of business and intellectual skills. In this new kind of Jewish community there would be celebration of the basis of life – self-sustaining, primary production, manual labour, an economic order that would be shared and egalitarian. I worked as well and as hard as I could, and I helped myself to what I needed from the kibbutz stores. Work without pay; a store without a cash desk; all you wanted to eat available in the *chederochel*. To ensure that this egalitarian reality should persist despite differences in family background and inequities that might flow from these, the children grew up in small collective units of their own, the Beit Sheil-halodim, the Children's Houses.

Here, in groups of five or six each, they were provided with safety, comfort, nannies and carers who would always be alert to how they were feeling and, even in the night, would be there to help. Each house had its little dining room and a small classroom for the first school lessons. Children were placed in one of these houses soon after they were born and grew up there until they could live independent lives. The distance between the Beit Sheil-halodim and the kibbutzniks' homes was no more than a hundred yards. There was always a back and forth. Parents could work long hours each day and not worry about who would take care of their children, and the children would see and know their parents as much as was possible within this collectivised system. It was an uncompromising attempt at utopia.

———

At the end of the first week of work I had a free day. I walked out from the cluster of kibbutz buildings, past a warehouse, towards the dunes and the sea.

The southern side of the kibbutz lands reached the border of the Gaza Strip. Three miles beyond this border, down the coast, was the Palestinian city of Gaza. Its buildings were not visible from the

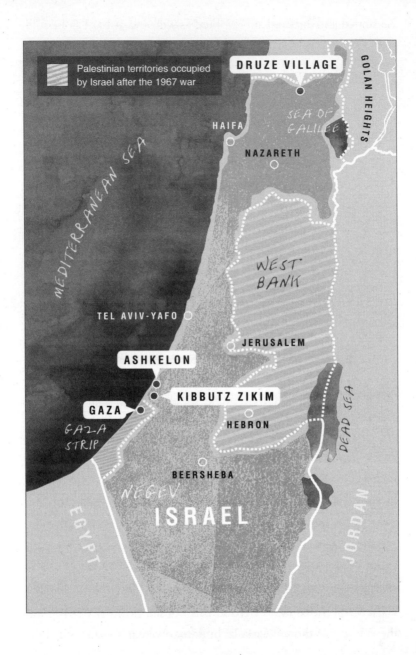

Palestinian territories occupied by Israel after the 1967 war

DRUZE VILLAGE

GOLAN HEIGHTS

SEA OF GALILEE

HAIFA

NAZARETH

MEDITERRANEAN SEA

WEST BANK

TEL AVIV-YAFO

JERUSALEM

ASHKELON

KIBBUTZ ZIKIM

DEAD SEA

GAZA

HEBRON

GAZA STRIP

BEERSHEBA

NEGEV

ISRAEL

EGYPT

JORDAN

Zikim side of the sand dunes, but at night I had watched multitudes of tiny flickering lights. Arieh had told me that these were the boats of the Palestinian fishermen who cast nets inshore, using flares in the dark to attract shoals of fish to within their reach. I had been told to be sure not to walk too far in that direction, for fear of finding myself in the border zone, and had been warned that the rise and fall of the dunes offered a concealed way for 'Arab infiltrators' to get from Gaza to Ashkelon – with the implication that anyone making this forbidden journey would be doing so for nefarious reasons.

I wanted to see the beach, and thought perhaps I would swim. Being sure not to head to the south, I followed a path that led towards a grove of trees, then, walking through these trees, I saw an old building, more or less a ruin. No doors or windows, but walls and, at one end, a roof in place. Everything was overgrown, neglected, unlike anything else on the kibbutz; as if someone had wanted to establish a zone of transition, between the homes set up on the desert and the sand dunes of the shoreline. I walked into the building, and saw that it had a tiled floor and hints of wrecked elegance – fine stonework where the walls and remains of tiles had not collapsed, the shapes of arched window spaces, and along one wall an inset stone seat. This was a building that pre-dated the kibbutz, and looked to have been an Arab home. At one end someone had piled a load of sacks – storage for the kibbutz farm, I guessed. I sat on the bench for a while, in the cool of its stone and tiles, looking out through the empty windows. I could see two lines of pomegranates, and grape vines. The outlines of a garden and orchard.

I felt an urge to explore the remains of the gardens, and wanted to see if any of the pomegranates, a few of them startlingly red on the trees, might be ripe. I pushed my way through high grasses and vines to pull down the fruit. Breaking it open I found the seeds, but they were dry and hard. A few grapes were soft and ripe; I broke off a bunch and walked on through the garden, which soon became the rough grasses and sand of the dunes. Then onto the beach, and to the sea. Lines of breakers were rolling up to the shore; I was amazed to see large fish leaping from the sides of waves. I had no idea what species they were – nothing familiar – but they were a sign that this was a place for fishing, and a remind-er of those boats from Gaza that sparkled at night. I turned and looked along the shore – to my left, the other side of the border, a few miles to the south, hidden beyond the dunes, were the houses of Gaza. Five miles to the north was Ashkelon. Two cities from the Bible. Samson and Delilah; the land of the Philistines. Behind me was the Arab house with its tiles and orchard. A triangle of far-off times. I was somewhere that was not Israel; the kibbutz a very new thing, laid out on the surface of this ancient landscape.

I pulled off my clothes and waded into the water, walked out into the surf. The water was warm and I swam out past the breakers. The waves flung me up and down; half swimming, half floating, I looked back at the long beach, the dunes and tried to make out the tops of the trees of the Arab orchard. I was alone, very far away from all I had ever known before, filled with feel-ings of relief. As I waded back to the beach, I stopped and turned to look out to the horizon, and wondered if it might be possible to cast a line, catch some of the leaping fish. I felt filled with every kind of possibility. A promised land.

I was befriended by some of the kibbutzniks, among them Motke, a man in his thirties who lived in Zikim with his English wife Miriam and their small children. He was an impassioned pacifist and a fierce enthusiast about the writings of George Bernard Shaw. He managed the banana groves and suggested that I become his assistant. I was delighted. My tasks would include weeding, cutting down trees that had fruited, moving drainage pipes, even driving the tractor, and from time to time helping with harvesting and loading the huge bunches of ripe fruit: everything that a banana plantation required. Sometimes the work would be hard, but, he said, there was always time to talk. For Motke the life of the mind, especially the puzzles of political philosophy, were at least as important as the bananas. He soon had me reading Bernard Shaw, explained to me over and over again the basic principles of Marxism and told me that the whole history of Israel was not as it seemed to be.

Motke had been a paratrooper in the 1956 Suez war, dropped beyond the front lines of the Israeli army as it advanced into the Sinai and, after fierce fighting, encircled sections of the Egyptian army. He described this military strategy, with all its risks for the paratroops and the way small groups of Israeli military found themselves taking many Egyptian prisoners. Motke recalled that he had been with a group of Israeli soldiers who executed their prisoners. He was horrified at the time, he said, and had never been able to forget, to get it out of his mind. This experience of war, his time as a front-line fighter in the Israeli army, had convinced him that the only way for a Jew to live in Israel was as a pacifist. The one hope, he told me many times, lay with the creation of a society in which Jews and Arabs shared a joint socialist dream. And he taught me how to manage banana trees.

Thus in the banana plantation, midway between Ashkelon and Gaza, I began to understand that events, and the accounts of events that become history, can be made to appear and disappear. I did not lose all my provincial naivety, nor overcome the tangle of confusions of my post-war childhood, but I became stronger, was burned brown, developed proud calluses on my hands, and learned a great deal. The men and women of the kibbutz, artists and urban refugees who had become farm workers, people living out their principles, were not Jews in any of the ways I had known Judaism. They did not seem to carry any of the burdens of Jewish identity. Perhaps the appearance of the absence of Jewishness came from the simple fact that here, for the first time in my life, I was in a society where everyone was a Jew. For people like Motke, being a Jew was either an irrelevance or something that they were keen to disregard – if to be a Jew meant believing in the God of the Old Testament, following a huge set of Talmudic rules and regulations, then it was not for them. And if it meant having an unqualified loyalty to everything that the state of Israel said and did, that was not for them either.

———————

Many of those I met at Zikim, including Motke, were – as I was – children of survivors of the Holocaust. But they did not explain Israel, nor their having chosen to live on a kibbutz, as a response to the trauma of the war. In his many accounts of modern Jewish history, and in the telling of his own story, Motke did not see Israel as an essential sanctuary. For him, as for all who talked to me about Israel, the kibbutz within the flow of world politics was a project for socialism rather than nationhood. The ideal was equality at least as much as homeland. The Holocaust of course had shaped their lives, their destinies, but for those kibbutzniks, in 1962, it was nowhere near the centre of their politics.

My grandmother had told me, in her whispering way, about a cousin of hers who had been in the Dachau and Buchenwald concentration camps, and had survived them both. His wife had sold everything they owned – their house in Berlin, all the contents of the house – and paid over all that she could scrape together to buy her husband's release. This was in the 1930s, before the 'final solution', when in the first phase of the anti-Jewish measures of Hitler's regime, the Nazis were keen to squeeze all the money they could from Jewish families. The couple were Bob and Tosca Rubel; after his release from the camps, they made their way to Palestine. They were still living there, in Tel Aviv. My grandmother and mother both hoped that I would go and visit them. It was a way for me to get to see Tel Aviv, they said. They sent a letter to Bob and Tosca to tell them I was going to be in Israel. They had sent me an invitation to come any time.

After my first month at Zikim, I was ready for a break from kibbutz work, and a chance to discover the new urban Israel. It was April 1962. I got the bus from Ashkelon to Tel Aviv and made my way to the building where Bob and Tosca Rubel lived. There was no street-level security, so I walked through the entrance to the small apartment block and up a flight of narrow stairs to the second floor, found their door and knocked.

Bob let me in. Tosca stood a short distance behind him in a tiny entrance hall. He was of medium height; she was much smaller. They both looked worn and stooped, their faces smiling at me in a mixture of excitement and uncertainty. They took my hands, shouted all manner of welcome in their broken English, and pulled me into their kitchen which was also their living room. It was furnished with a table with four chairs around it, an armchair at the other side of the room, some bookcases, and not much else. A sink below a narrow window, and, to one side, a cooker. It was a very small flat. I was to discover that they had lived there for many years, in great simplicity. They had never had children, and seemed to have very little contact with anyone. This apartment, set out with only the essentials, contained them. I was happy to meet them, warmed by their obvious excitement to be welcoming me, but I felt uneasy, an intruder on this small space.

Within minutes of my arriving, sitting at their kitchen table, they started to talk about their lives, their escape. Tosca told the part of the story I had heard from my grandmother, the taking of Bob, first to Dachau; his being transferred to Buchenwald, though she did not know why and could only fear the worst. The knowledge that he could be bought out of there for a price, that the price was everything they had: their home, their bank accounts, their savings, their silver. They had been middle class, comfortable, part of the assimilated Jewish community, had thought they were Austrians living in Germany, that they were safe. It had been sudden, unbelievable. At first the only thought was how to save Bob's life, and then how to get away. They had nothing, they said, but in a way there was no such thing as nothing if you feared death, if being alive was what you could achieve. They were lucky – to live, to be able to make their way to Palestine. That was the one possible sanctuary. They told me that they had never thought of going there, but there was, for them at that time, nowhere else.

I sat in the cramped kitchen of a tiny flat in a drab area of Tel Aviv, and for the first time was taken by members of my family to the stories that had delivered their destiny; the stories in which I could hear and imagine the forces, states of mind, decisions that, in some other part of Europe, along another line of escape, but with the same fears, my mother and grandmother had made their way to the safety of the north of England. They had made a life in Sheffield, and I had been born into that life. Bob and Tosca had made a new life for themselves in Tel Aviv. They took me to the circumstances that caused them to be in this city, this country, as the starting point, as the way of introducing themselves to me. With an explanation of how they came to be alive at all despite the camps, they welcomed me to their home.

Bob and Tosca must have been in their mid-sixties, but appeared to be much older. They were brittle with nerves. Tosca sometimes trembled when she spoke, which was with a quiet, almost reluctant voice; Bob was much more outgoing, with a nervous, troubled energy. Yet both of them were unfailingly welcoming and generous. I was a messenger from the side of the family now living in England, whom they almost never saw. And I was young, the new generation. They had no children; for many of our relatives, the war put an end to the possibility of children. So I was given every treat that they could offer.

They cooked Central European food for me, told me more stories about their lives and took me to hear the famous Israeli Philharmonic Orchestra. They loved music, especially Beethoven. Bob's delight during a concert at times would be too much for him to contain: as a favourite section or phrase was about to be played he would lean close to me, begin tapping on my shoulder and would whisper into my ear: 'Here it comes, here it comes, da daa, dum di daa. Listen, listen, *now!*' And the piece of music he loved would be played while he murmured to me.

Bob also wanted to talk to me about Adolf Eichmann, the man who was a monster, who had organised the transport of Jews to the camps. I had never heard of Eichmann. I sat in the tiny flat in Tel Aviv and was given a first lesson in modern Jewish history. Bob told the story as he had heard it, showing what it meant to him – adding his own small questions or challenges. It began with Eichmann hiding in Argentina – how could they have let him get away to Argentina? Then a report to Israeli intelligence, or to those searching for the worst of the Nazi war criminals – they will never stop looking for the murderers. Eichmann was sighted in Buenos Aires, a tip-off that seems to have originated from a girlfriend of Eichmann's son Klaus. The girlfriend came from a half-Jewish family – didn't they know she was Jewish? She told her father; he alerted authorities in West Germany. Israeli agents were sent to Argentina. They watched the Eichmann house and followed him. They learned that each day he took a bus; so they waited for him at the bus stop, seized him, took him prisoner – but how could they get him to Israel? They filled him with drugs, disguised him as a flight attendant, and got him onto an El Al plane – and now they could make him stand in a court.

Bob spoke of all this in a hoarse whisper, as if any loud exclamation of his relief that the murderer was captured might cause this good news to be stolen and enable the Nazis to take their Eichmann back to safety. I listened as if this was all a secret they were sharing with me.

The search for Adolf Eichmann and the story of his arrest in 1961 were the starting point for a restatement, a form of rediscovery, of Jewish modern history. It came to be a story, a flow of events and stories behind events, that changed the story of Israel and even the very meaning of Judaism. The trial was set up as a reckoning with, and a refusal to accept, post-war silences. Over a hundred witnesses gave evidence for the prosecution, a horrifying stream of personal testimony that lasted four months. On 12 December Eichmann was found not guilty of personally killing anyone, but guilty of being a central figure in the Nazis' mass murder and plans for genocide. Three days later, on 15 December, he was sentenced to death. He was due to be hanged in May of the following year – just two months after my arrival in Israel.

For Bob and Tosca the trial was a chance for the world to know, so I must know; or they must share knowledge with me so they could be heard and understood as perhaps they had never had a chance to be heard before. I was given a role in the drama so that the trial became a new event within the walls of their apartment. I sat with them and listened and of course they asked me, perhaps in a rhetorical way: what did I think? What could the young think? I did not have any answers; what made sense to me was to listen, and to read each day some details from the trial.

A central and troubling question that the trial still had to deal with was the death sentence. Eichmann had been found guilty as a mass murderer, but was he to be executed? In Israel, at that time, this would mean his being hanged. Appeals and arguments were being reported every day. Bob and Tosca asked me what I thought about this. Thus far, at that kitchen table, I had been very quiet, had asked questions to hear more of their stories. But I spoke with some energy against death sentences, and therefore against the hanging even of Eichmann. A matter of principle, stated with all the dogmatic conviction that could be achieved by a teenager who had for the first time discovered political principle, and had been spending time on a Mapam kibbutz under the influence of a pacifist follower of George Bernard Shaw. My sweet and vulnerable hosts went silent. I saw that they were both very upset; Bob began to shake. Tosca consoled him. I stopped speaking. There was a long pause. The three of us at that little table. Then Bob said, in a trembling voice, 'You cannot understand, could not understand.' He continued to shake. Tosca held his hands, murmured to him some calming words, more sounds than words. His head swung from side to side.

He said again, 'You don't know.' And something at the core of us was revealed to me, a reality that my family had never allowed me to see but which I had known about as a residue within myself – the anguish that their history, that history itself, the war, the fear, the deaths, had caused in them. It was unbearable; so they had fled from it all to Tel Aviv.

I went back to the kibbutz.

When the bananas needed to be watered, we would begin work at three in the morning. Motke would drive me out to the groves on the huge old tractor, and set up the network of pipes and taps to begin the watering well before dawn so that the water could flow before evaporating in the heat of the day.

About two months after I began work with Motke the calm of this routine was disrupted: a detachment of the Israeli army arrived, setting up camp between the kibbutz and Ashkelon, somewhere on the dunes, out of sight, at the margin of the kibbutz lands. We were told that there was a new concern about security along the border. The army was going to create traps for Arab 'infiltrators'.

One early morning as Motke drove us in the dark to begin the irrigation work, we were suddenly lit up by powerful floodlights being beamed at us from an invisible vehicle: dazzled by the glare, we could see nothing beyond where we sat on the tractor. A voice ordered us to keep driving. It was an Israeli army patrol, making sure we were not Arab infiltrators, reminding us that the army was in control, even in the dark, on the track from the kibbutz to the banana plantation.

A few days later Motke was summoned to a meeting. The military unit was concerned about the safety of those who were driving tractors out to the bananas in the darkness before dawn. Motke was told that there were Arab infiltrators coming through the dunes near the bananas; we must be ready to defend ourselves; we should be armed. He was given an Uzi, the famous Israeli-made machine gun, small and deadly. The next morning, he came to pick me up as usual to head out to do the irrigating. He parked the tractor by the hut where I stayed, climbed down and handed me the Uzi. He would not use it, he said, and preferred not to carry a gun. Motke reminded me that he was a pacifist. I should do whatever defending of us might be necessary. I must have told him that I had owned a shotgun or some stories about shooting ducks or pheasants in the English countryside. Enough to entitle him to say that this Uzi was for me to hold and, if necessary, to use. And enough for me to be too embarrassed to admit that I had very little idea of how this unfamiliar and alarming weapon worked. I took it, slung it over my shoulder, and carried it each time thereafter that we drove in the dark to the bananas. I am not sure I even knew where the safety catch was. Motke never showed me. But we were doing as the Israeli military demanded: we were armed.

It was unclear what we were armed against. There was a good deal of fear of 'Arabs', and the news that there were infiltrators moving from the Egyptian side of the Gaza Strip towards Ashkelon caused some anxiety among the kibbutzniks. Yet just about everyone was full of scepticism about the military, and all were opposed to the national government – this was a Mapam kibbutz, part of the early socialist Zionist movement that was critical of much that Israel's government of the day was saying and doing. Scepticism about right-wing Zionism, however, did not mean that the kibbutz was or felt safe. Infiltrators were enemies, even if it was not quite clear of whom. The kibbutz did sit on land that had been acquired from a Palestinian family, and kibbutzniks said they had paid a fair price for it. Motke suspected that the original owner, who had been a minister in the last Palestinian administration before the 1948 war, would not have agreed. So there was a degree of insecurity and fear.

I was caught up in the generalised anxiety, but was protected from it by Motke's refusal to yield to the idea of violence. The gun in my hand was a gesture that was required. I accepted my role as holder of the Uzi and took a kind of incompetent responsibility for at least appearing to be able to fight off the invisible, lurking enemy by whom we might at any moment be ambushed in the dark. Yet it was the principles Motke advocated that gave us our sense of safety: we were not part of the nation's militarism. We chugged along on the tractor, in the 3 a.m. darkness, heading out to the bananas to do the irrigation. Motke drove; I stood behind him, clinging to the mudguard rail, the Uzi I did not know how to use hanging from my shoulder. From time to time we would again be lit up by the headlights of an Israeli military jeep that had appeared from a concealed place along our route – checking up on who we were, and then making sure we were armed. This flash of light would always send a shock of fear through me.

Not long after we began to carry the Uzi an order came for a large quantity of bananas. We had to commit all our time to the harvest. Much of the fruit was ripe, and we spent a long day cutting bunches and piling them on a flat-bed towed by the tractor up and down the tracks that divided the plantation into blocks of trees. By mid-afternoon the stack of bunches was high, and we were close to the end of the job.

The tractor and trailer were moving along the last track, which separated the western side of the plantation from the dunes that then merged into the beach. There were three of us at work – Motke, Gershon, a young South African who had been living on the kibbutz for a few weeks, and me. Motke was sitting in the tractor's driving seat; Gershon and I were carrying the last bunches of bananas to the cart. Suddenly there was a loud explosion. A gun, someone must be shooting at us. Gershon shouted out in fear, and as a warning: '*Aravim, Aravim.*' Arabs. He and I dived for cover. We lay down under a few trees a little way into the plantation, hoping to be invisible to any sniper hidden in the dunes beyond the tractor and trailer loaded with bananas. Motke, the resolute pacifist, insisted on staying on the tractor. Gershon called to him to take cover. After a minute or two of silence – no more shots – Motke climbed down with a self-conscious refusal to be hurried. He walked the long way round the back of the trailer, looking towards the dunes, as open as could be to snipers, as if to find an Arab he could discuss things with. Gershon and I stayed cowering among the trees.

Motke came round to our side of the trailer and called out to us. It's OK, no problem. A flat. A flat? What was he talking about? We emerged from the banana trees. Yes, a flat. One of the tyres on the trailer had burst with a bang; the weight of bananas had been too much for it. There were no Aravim.

———————

Another couple from my grandmother's family had also escaped to Palestine, Gania and Avner Badian. They had emigrated from Poland before the war and I knew nothing about them. They had been kept wrapped in even more silence than Bob and Tosca, though they were relatives through Hilel Badian, my grandmother's father, and the man after whom I had been given my Hebrew name. I had not even heard of them when I planned the trip to Israel; if they had ever visited England after the war, they had never been to our house, and had not found any place in the bits of family history that were told. But now that I was in Israel, my mother had asked me to visit them: they would be quite old, she said, an aging couple living in Haifa. She must have written to say that I was at Zikim. I received an invitation and was given an address. I took another break from the kibbtuz, got the bus to Haifa and, with the help of a city street plan, walked to the house from the bus station. It was a long way, and took me up one of the hills that rise to the north and east of the city, where some of the most generous suburban housing had already spread. As I walked I looked out on more and more of the city below, and to the sea beyond. It was a hot afternoon, but, after two months in Israel, I was well adjusted to heat and fit from the labour on the kibbutz. The walk was a pleasure; Haifa is a city of great beauty.

I found the house. It was, like almost all the houses around it, low and white with a small but heavily planted garden. Mr and Mrs Badian were waiting for me, though they can't have known what time I might arrive. They welcomed me into a living room made dark with heavy furniture that crowded the space, and with windows half covered against the sunlight. Gania was frail and quiet – she did not speak English, and we did our best in German and French – but Avner was full of restless energy and spoke to me in rapid, fluent English. I was given a cup of something to drink, offered food, and quizzed. Question after question about the family and about what I was doing in Israel. Why a kibbutz? Why Mapam? What did I do there? I was given little time to answer. Gania was silent, and Avner seemed troubled and discomfited, somehow sceptical, or even a little hostile. I had no way to understand what might have been at work in them, in this dark room.

Even after the experience of Bob and Tosca I did not know how I should behave, and my appearance may have upset them. They were from the Central European middle classes, the grand bourgeoisie of wealthy assimilated Jews in the Austro-Hungarian Empire. I was an unkempt eighteen year old who had taken the bus from a socialist kibbutz, then walked in the heat up the hill. I must have been dishevelled and sweaty. There were unpleasant sores on one of my hands – a cut that had become infected. I carried no more than a carrier bag of essentials. Not at all what they might have expected; not at all what they might have wanted. I began to suspect that they were on the other side of various ideological divides, opposed to the socialist project I appeared to have joined. They may well have wanted no reminders and messengers from the past; may have felt a tumult of inner difficulty at my arrival; or may have needed to know all that could not be known – what had happened to everyone they had lost, or lost contact with, in the last twenty years. Little wonder that Avner charged at me, quizzed me, had difficulty with my being there.

At one point I found myself standing at a bay window of their house, looking out over shrubs and gardens that fell away down the steep hillside towards the sea. My eyes caught the movements of birds flitting about in the plants in front of the window. Avner saw me notice them. 'So,' he challenged, 'what are those birds? Do you know what those birds are?'

I was surprised by his tone but relieved by the question. I had noticed two different species, one hovering by some flowers, the other darting among the shrubs. A Palestinian sunbird and an African bulbul, I said. He was taken aback and, for the first time since I had arrived, somewhat pleased. I knew the names of the birds; something that he valued, so perhaps I was not as bad as I appeared. His manner towards me changed a little. Later that afternoon he asked me if I played chess. Yes, I said, Oma, my grandmother, Mrs Schäfer, had taught me. I did not mention that the chess set we had always played on was the one that had belonged to Hilel Badian; no doubt it would have been a set he had played on himself when visiting the Badian home in Lvov. We played a long, complicated game.

The darkness of that home in the bright suburbs of Haifa was, of course, a darkness from Europe, a way of being in its shades, in Israel but not quite there, not all that far from an original Jewish home, in Vienna or Lvov. I was invited into that home in Haifa because I was a member of a family that Europe had whittled down to a few isolated households, scattered in the places they had found to survive. Two Badians in Haifa, the aging couple in Tel Aviv – households without children, where no children ever visited. A place of survival and, I suspect, anguish. A home where there was nothing much to do, and perhaps nothing that they wanted to say, to remember. And here I was, the next generation, a survivor in my own way. I would never have thought of myself in those terms, but in that gloomy house I felt a familiar mix of belonging and being alien.

I was a European by heritage and, in many ways, by virtue of what I had been taught: the lessons from my grandmother, her whispering voice, the Latin and speaking French, playing chess with her father's set. So I did belong to this part of the family, this piece of an old Central Europe in the new state of Israel, and I did belong in Israel, since I was a Jew and had been living on a kibbutz. But I did not belong, with my English looks and voice and enthusiasms. Even to know about birds, for all that it surprised my host into a begrudging respect, was a part of being a stranger – it came from immersion in England and Englishness. I saw myself as much an interloper as a welcome part of the family. In reality there was no family to be part of – not a geography of homes in which and through which relatives looked to one another for meaning and support. To look for family, even in Israel, was to experience its elusiveness, its disappearance. Unless Israel itself, with its claim to be the essential or ultimate homeland, is made into and seen as a social and psychic alternative to family, a replacement for families that were lost. In the dark home of the Badians I had a disturbing, even frightening feeling of being alive, perhaps too alive to be welcomed by these muted survivors.

Soon after getting back to the kibbutz, when the harvesting of the sweetcorn was nearly finished, a group of Israeli soldiers and their officer appeared at a field where the kibbutz's large combine was getting under way. The circle of standing corn was large, but turn by turn made larger by each round of cuts. The circle of corn was large, but turn by turn getting smaller. The officer insisted that there were Arab infiltrators hiding in that diminishing circle, and said they wanted to march into the crop and find them. The kibbutznik in charge of the combine said this was unacceptable – they would do great damage to a precious crop. Instead, the soldiers should wait by the field as the combine cut its way towards the centre; no one could leave the field without being seen. The combine continued to cut the corn, circling and tightening the circle. It did not take long for the corn to be reduced to a small round patch. Suddenly a group of men stood up, hands in the air. The officer had been right. As soon as they stood up, though, the soldiers shot them down.

The people of Zikim who had witnessed this violence were appalled. They helped the wounded, and filed a complaint with the Israeli army. Then, a few weeks later, an individual infiltrator was captured on the dunes and brought to the kibbutz. The soldiers who had brought him made him lie down on the ground with his hands behind his back; an Israeli officer bent over him to tie on a blindfold. As the blindfold was tightened over the man's eyes, he made a sudden movement with his hands. One of the soldiers shot him in the back: he said afterwards that he was afraid that the man might have had a knife hidden on him. Again the kibbutz was outraged, and filed another official complaint.

What did I make of these events, taking place where I lived? I talked about them with Motke, who insisted that this problem of 'infiltrators' was something Israel had brought on itself. The irony, or, to use his word, the contradiction, he said, was what we should be talking about. The kibbutz was on Palestinian land, or lands that Palestinians did not see as having been bought from them by Israel in ordinary transactions. But Palestinians who crossed this land, or moved along the beach and dunes alongside it, were feared and shot at. I did not know the history of land exchanges or appropriation in the area between Ashkelon and Gaza, but Motke knew a great deal about the history of the kibbutz and also the new nation as a whole. It's from 15 to 85 per cent, he would say. In 1947 Palestinians owned and occupied 85 per cent of the land that became Israel; by 1950 that had become 15 per cent. How had we managed to take all this land so fast? His point, the issue he kept raising again and again, as did so many of those who lived on the kibbutz, was that the Israeli state was at least in part to be held accountable for this tension, not just the 'infiltrators'. The questions Motke and others wanted to ask turned me towards regional history and politics. None of them believed that to criticise the Israeli state was to betray either Judaism or one or another version (sectarian, socialist, utopian even) of Zionism. On the contrary, as far as I understood, and as I was all the time being told, it was not just alright, it was politically and indeed morally essential to know and speak these truths.

————————

During my five months at Zikim I lived in a large one-room shack in a line of such shacks that had been put up for visitors and seasonal workers on the side of the kibbutz adjacent to the dunes. At first I had the room to myself; later I shared it with an American student who was suffering uncontrollable diarrhoea – a difficult few days. Then with another English visitor who was also between school and university. One of the neighbouring shacks was occupied by a group of three Druze Arabs, men from the Lebanese border area.

The Druze are an Arab community that is scattered between northern Palestine, Lebanon and Syria. Their religion is rooted in Islam but their political and social affiliations are surprising. Many Druze who lived and worked in Israel had taken positions in the Israeli army and were participants in many aspects of life in Israel. My neighbours had taken jobs on the kibbutz as guards. They were awake much of every night, taking turns to patrol the boundaries of the kibbutz and be on the look-out for 'infiltrators'. All night they would be listening to their continuous music, played on a crackling radio set, talking loudly and punctuating the sounds of music with startling expectoration – a gurgling clearing of the throat followed by a loud spit.

I was a little afraid of these strange men, speaking Arabic and making such a cacophony of unfamiliar sounds. They were not part of the community of kibbutzniks that I ate, visited and worked with. Although they were my neighbours, they lived to one side of everyone else, different, and other. Then one night, struggling to sleep, after a series of nights of having been woken or kept awake, my tiredness added to indignation and I stomped over to their place, knocked on the open door and did my best to protest.

I had anticipated hostility, but they seemed delighted to see me standing there at the door to their house, were full of apology and eager for me to come in and chat with them. They spoke a little bit of English and were determined we should become friends. From then on they were careful about the level of the noise they made, and I minded far less about it – coming to love the lilting, beautiful, relentless, mournful music. About a month later, the period of their work as guards came to an end. Before they left the kibbutz they told me that I must visit them in their village, up in the north. They would make me welcome any time. They gave me the address.

———

Towards the end of my stay on the kibbutz, my brother came to visit. We decided to rent a car and drive to some other parts of the country. Motke and his wife Miriam would come with us. I suggested that we drive up to the Lebanese border and visit the Druze who had been my neighbours. Some searching on maps showed us just where they were. I was filled with excitement about getting to the very edges of Israel. Motke had been making sure that I heard the Israeli political norms being interrogated by his anti-nationalist and socialist views. A chance to travel to a region, a social and actual landscape, that lay beyond the ideological boundaries of Israel, at its northern frontiers where Israel blurred with an Arab world, felt like a much needed adventure. Early in the morning, in the last week of July, we drove off.

We travelled through the middle of the country that lay between Ashkelon and Tel Aviv, and then left the densely occupied plains beyond Galilee; we climbed through the hills of northern Israel, driving through a landscape of narrow rocky gullies and hillsides covered with low scrub and olive groves. Twice we stopped at remote wooded canyons to look for wild grapes to pick and places we might be able to swim. At one of these, as we climbed down a slope of huge, gnarled olive trees and found a vine heavy with dark grapes, Motke suddenly called out, 'We have entered the Bible.' I felt the force of what he said: to be in this land, without any settlements or new towns, rough and timeless, was to feel alive in some elemental way. For the last part of the journey, climbing up into the hills towards the Lebanese border, we seemed to go further and further into this zone of some other geography and another time. Twice we were stopped by Israeli patrols, were questioned, and told that we should not think of driving on these roads at night. They were bemused to hear we were on our way to visit friends in one of the villages near the border, but they let us continue on our way.

At last, high in the hills, we came to the Druze village we were looking for. Its entrance was a stone arch, part of a wall around the lower part of the village. Through the arch, along a steep track that led further up the hillside, we could see a cluster of houses separated by narrow alleys and small patches of garden. As soon as we drove through the arch, children and young men came hurrying to the car. Motke knew some Arabic; he interpreted the flow of questions and instructions that greeted us. Who were we? Where were we going? Who were we looking for? Up there, that way! We did our best to explain, and gave the name of the Druze family we hoped to visit. There, that way! A group of boys led us up the hill, around a short hairpin bend, into the heart of the village, to the house. The track was narrow, with deep ruts and edged with loose rocks; opposite the door they pointed to a space just wide enough to fit a car without blocking the track.

As we climbed out, children gathered round the car. One of my former neighbours came rushing out of the doorway. He was delighted to see us, urging us to come in and be made welcome. He told us not to worry about the car; they would tell some of the children to make sure it was safe. He showed us into his house. There was a kitchen area through an open door to the left of a small, dark and cool hallway; then a room beyond with a table, chairs, rugs, a large radio and windows where fierce sunlight shone through very thin and worn mesh curtains.

My neighbour, followed by another man and some boys, led us into the further room, while the women, veiled and shy, prepared food for us in the kitchen. We managed to talk in broken English and with some help from Motke's Arabic. The women passed through small cups of very strong coffee, glasses of water, plates piled with pieces of different varieties of melon and then bowls of Turkish delight. I remember little of what we talked about, though there was a long story about the British army – one of the men in the family had been in the British infantry during the war and then, in Jerusalem, during the 1948 conflict.

Most of all I remember the feeling of welcome and fascination. I wanted to know everything about this village – how they lived, what the crops were that we could see in the gardens and in fields beyond the houses and the wall. I had left the territories I had known, the places where I had been led to expect to feel at home. By not being in any version of my promised lands, I found that I was unexpectedly, intensely alive. I did not know that this was to be a first discovery of what would become a heartland of my life, a feeling of homecoming among strangers.

A QUESTION OF SILENCE

My brother and I left Israel together. We decided to take a ferry from Haifa to the Greek island of Rhodes, stay there for a while, then get the train from Athens to London. He had romantic reasons for visiting Athens; I was in no hurry to be back in England. The ferry to Rhodes was small. The journey would take a day and a night, but there were no cabins, or none that we could afford. Passengers crowded onto the deck, looking for a place to settle down and, if possible, sleep. We found a spot, near the bow of the ship, and squeezed up against others. There were many young people, like ourselves, leaving Israel for their homes in northern Europe, and there were Greek peasant families, camped out on the deck with their many bags of produce that they had bought and were carrying home as trade. Everyone had brought with them food, which they shared or swopped, making for a twenty-four-hour picnic. I may have imagined it, or it might have been just my own strong feeling, but I sensed that there was intense and shared relief to be leaving Israel.

This feeling was reinforced by a long encounter with one of the passengers crowded alongside us. He was a tall and dark-skinned man of about thirty; he spoke fluent English, but it was hard to place his accent. Not from England, nor from America, he gave guttural quality to his consonants, much as people from Central Europe do who have learned English as children but use non-English sounds. As well as sounding unlike the other young men and women on the boat, he appeared to be travelling very much alone. Pressed into such close proximity, we found ourselves talking to him. He did not seem to want to chat, but we asked the obvious questions. Had he been in Israel a long time? A while, he said, a good amount of time. And was he Israeli? Why do you ask? he said. Does it matter to you if I am Israeli or not? I was confused and uncomfortable. And would it matter if I were Palestinian? Am I what I say I am or what you think I am? He confronted us with these terse and rather hostile responses to our queries. I don't remember many of his exact words, except that he challenged us with thoughts about identity.

What is important to you? Where I say I come from or what I believe in? Would you be more friendly to me if I were Israeli, or Arab? Or if I told you I was a socialist? These were not questions to which I could give any answers. I realised I was being confronted. Only now, many years later, do I think back to that young man and his challenges, understanding how much anger they contained and the possible causes for bitterness that lay behind them.

———————

On coming back from Israel I wanted to talk with my family about the Eichmann trial, the shock of the evidence and the argument with Bob and Tosca about the death sentence. What was the testimony that could have come from our family? Where had our relatives died? And who were the Badians? How did they fit into the family? I was given a few clichés and dismissive banalities about the relatives in Israel – aren't they odd? What narrow lives they have led. How sad they didn't have children. I hope they made you welcome; well, I am sure they did.

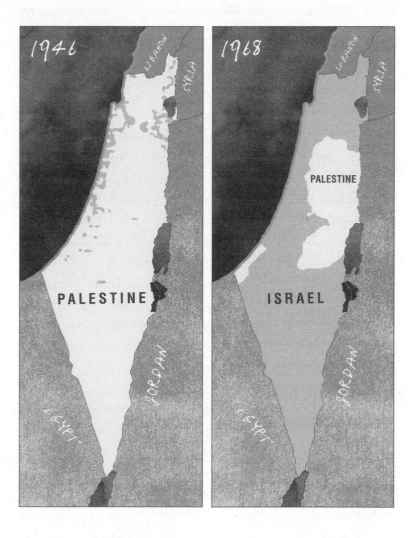

Apart from this disengaged interest my mother insisted that there was no point in asking these questions, better to leave it alone. What is to be said? Don't speak about it. She did not say that it was too painful for her, or too exposing. And anyway, I would not have understood either her pain or her fear of exposure.

A consequence of silence is the absence of sympathy for silence. I did not have the words in which to think about the way my mother found her place, made her family as English as possible. To search for her family's testimony, the details they could have added to the case for the prosecution at the trial in Jerusalem, would have subverted her, and taken her back to the places she had devoted herself to escaping. Her task was to ensure that her escape was complete.

The brief, even cold rebuttal of my questions matched her own need to stay away from the terrible details, the markers of all that she needed to bury as far out of sight as possible. I sat with her and my father in the sitting room of the house in Sheffield, everything as it had been since my brother and I were small children. I needed to tell them what I had seen, to let them hear my thoughts spoken alongside theirs, to hear them place themselves in the story of Israel. If Israel was indeed the place they believed in. But there were no answers, no memories, just confusing and kindly evasions. To speak to what it meant would mean entering, re-entering, the territories from which they had escaped. If Israel was important to them, it was as an idea, an image of escape. I heard this in their voices and their lack of voice, and was left with the silence.

———

Israel faded to the back of my mind. Being a student at Oxford and then going to work in Ireland, I took many steps away from that set of experiences, though the ideals of the Mapam kibbutz lived on – in me and, I believed, in the world. Then it was May 1967. The media were filled with alarming news: Israel was at risk of being destroyed. Egypt had taken a series of measures to squeeze Israel. Then it closed the Suez Canal to all Israeli shipping and ships headed for Israel; steps to subvert the Israeli economy and weaken the Jewish state. It evoked the Nazi measures to constrict Jewish life in the 1930s, the first steps towards the Holocaust. Around the world Jews – and I was one of them – felt shocks of terror.

At the same time Arab forces were being massed on the Egyptian borders in Sinai and Gaza. Tanks dug into positions with their guns facing into Israel. Arab leaders were putting out statements to the effect that the time had come for a final reckoning with the state of Israel: it had to be removed from the political map; it must be destroyed. Newspapers printed terrifying statements of intent, and ran aggressive and bellicose quotes from Arab leaders – particularly from Nasser, long-time president of Egypt, whose 1965 declaration that 'we aim at the destruction of Israel' had been part of a long rhetoric of defiance of the alliance, as he saw it, of Israel and the imperial powers of the world against Arab interests. We were being warned by the media and by political voices in Europe and the United States that Israel's existence was under threat and that we should fear for a massacre of its population.

The unanimity and anxiety in the media were intense. All that I had been inspired by in Israel seemed to be in ultimate danger. What I had learned from the 1961 Eichmann trial was that this danger evoked the murder of the Jews in Europe less than thirty years before. These were the stories that gave purpose to Israel, and flashes of both pain and recovery from pain to my family. The actors in a geopolitical drama were drawn in vivid form: Jewish survivors of the camps, those who had managed to escape, were again surrounded by an enemy whose intent was their destruction. David faced with Goliath. Thus was the argument made, and thus did it echo in me. I was filled with an unexpected, overwhelming sense of alarm.

As the crisis built at the very end of May and in the first days of June, the Israeli Embassy in London announced that it would welcome volunteers to give whatever service they could in defence of beleaguered Israel. To my own surprise, I felt a desperate fear that Israel could be at risk. So the stories had reached me, either through my grandmother's whispering or Bob and Tosca's anxious voices. The questions Motke had asked and the unspoken anger of the young man on the boat to the Greek islands sank out of sight. I went to London, to the Embassy. I would volunteer; there must be something I could do, rather than just pace up and down and read all the news bulletins I could find. I stood in a long queue of young men and women at the Embassy and was given an interview. What was my job? I was a lecturer in social philosophy. Did I speak languages other than English? Yes, I said. They asked some simple questions in French, German and Hebrew. I managed to give some simple answers. The interview lasted about five minutes. I had a strong impression that I was just the sort of person they did not want to meet. They would be in touch, they said. I never heard from them.

The events of what came to be called the Six Day War are well known. At the time they were a drama that unfolded almost hour by hour, news bulletin to news bulletin. On 5 June we learned that Israel had launched a surprise aerial bombardment, aimed first at the Egyptian air force. This was followed by reports of similar attacks in Syria and Jordan. By the end of 9 June the media could be sure that there was no longer resistance to Israeli advance positions from any of the segments of the Arab armies. On 10 June Israel declared a ceasefire. Reports of casualties followed, and were full of imprecision. Somewhere between 20,000 and 50,000 Arab soldiers had been killed – estimates were coming from opposing interests. In spite of the enormity of Goliath, the newspapers declared, David, in the form of the Israel Defence Forces, had occupied an area that was three times the size of the 1948 land of Israel. Soon other numbers were being spoken of: about 400,000 Palestinians had been displaced – most fleeing as refugees into neighbouring states. At least a million Palestinians were now living within the ceasefire borders.

For those few days the world stared at, responded to, examined the reports from the front lines, the drama of the Israeli demolition of the Arab armies and its occupation of huge areas of Arab territory, swathes of Palestinian land. I listened to the radio, bought every edition of the *Evening Standard*, focused on these events. At first I felt afraid – for Israel, for the ideal of the kibbutz, for the people whose agonies had been set out in the course of the Eichmann trial, and at Bob and Tosca's kitchen table – there were many reasons for holding to the Zionist project. Defeat was unthinkable.

Yet as soon as the extent and nature of the Israeli military victories became clear, I felt unsure. About the origins of this war, the stories by which it had been surrounded and justified, and the implications for the future. Was this a defensive action or part of a long-worked-out plan to increase the size of Israel? Had this set up a new basis for a settlement with Palestinians, or was it a huge increment in the extent of Palestinian losses? Was this colonial expansion, a seizing and settling of Palestinian villages and lands, or a temporary occupation that might provide bargaining power, leverage that won some of the security Israel said it needed in exchange for a return to the pre-war borders?

These questions, or set of anxieties, began to challenge, once again but with a new force, my view of Israel. The answers that were given to the questions, the way events unfolded, became a turning point, a shift in perspective, that became ever more disturbing and ever more inescapable. As Israel declared that it would never yield up its total control of Jerusalem and allowed new Jewish settlements to be built on the conquered territories, I felt dismay and outrage. Much of Sinai was yielded up, but not Gaza; the front line moved back in Syria, but not from the Golan Heights. And the entire West Bank, with its many Palestinian villages, became a colonial territory. Israel was in military occupation of Gaza and the West Bank: the opportunity this created for redefining the country on the basis of mutual recognition – the Arab world of Israel, Israel of the Palestinians – was there and being lost. Lost because, it more and more seemed to me, it had never been a part of any plan.

The 1967 war changed everything. The opportunity of victory was not taken. Israel was occupying, as an invading enemy, lands that had been defined as Palestinian as part of the deal from which Israel had emerged. Demands for a return to the pre-1967 borders became a call for moderation and some form of justice and the genesis of ever more violence. To watch the events unfold in the West Bank and Gaza, to see the Arab world in its own collusion with the dispossession of those who had fled to the refugee camps, was to discover layers of injustice and brutality. For many hundreds of thousands of Jews, as for multitudes of non-Jews who had supported Israel after 1948, the politics became a personal night-mare. A surprising thought began to shape in my mind, in many Jewish minds: the great achievement of Judaism, for my kind of family, was its commitment to what it deemed to be civilisation – thought, letters, music, art, humanitarian skills, the great professional avocations. Thus the reasons for taking pride in our heritage were at odds with colonial aggression. The Judaism I had been brought up on did not rely on myths about deities, but, instead, at its best, celebrated the truths of culture. Not a religion so much as a way of looking at and being in the world, and therefore alert to the dangers of this expanding, aggressive, triumphant Israel. There germinated the realisation that to be a Jew may in some profound ways mean a disassociation from Israel. What was I to make of this new conquest, and the fierce resistance to it that was appropriate and inevitable? All Jews were welcome there; that was in its view of itself as a new nation, meeting an historic need. But Judaism, from its core, its place in the history of civilisation, might none-theless imply, entail even, criticism of Israel. There was always one simple question that lay behind and within the argument: how could a nation created to shelter the persecuted and provide a land to the dispossessed engage in the persecution and dispossession of others? Yet this question kept being shrouded in silence. I began to see that there could well be a moral and conceptual gap between Judaism and Zionism.

Many of the Jews I knew, including my father's sister and brother-in-law, said they wanted to go to Israel. They would have gone if they could; so much prevented them from going. What was this

Israel? An imagined sanctuary, the land of the forefathers, a place to be or to imagine being. A territory where at least some of the family could be safe – and knowing that this 'family' might be those most closely related, the men and women and children tied to us by blood, or it might be all who were Jews and tied to us by the blood that has been spilled in torrents in modern history.

The insistence on Jewishness in my family may have taken its language from Talmudic teachings – not to eat pork or shellfish, to say some Hebrew prayers on a Friday evening, to have a great banquet of a Seder night on the first evenings of the Passover, or not to marry non-Jews. These rulings or habits or preferences or anxieties – it is hard to say what they had been – sound like dictates from Jewish law. And when they came from my father, and his father who grew up in a *shtetl* in Eastern Europe, with his background in the Sheffield Jewish community, the rules could indeed be echoes of Talmudic law.

But for my family, to be a Jew was to have been defined and shaped and traumatised by the events of the twentieth century, the shadows of the camps. Israel, or the Zionist visions from which it took shape, had a history before the Holocaust. And the Holocaust has been denied or minimised without reference to Israel. But the Israel that I heard about and grew up to imagine, and went to live in, took its shape from the events of 1933–45, from the rise of the Nazis to their defeat. It fulfilled the need that Primo Levi expressed with greater clarity and passion than any other writer: Israel had to exist because of the war, the mass murder, and because there must never be silence about the Holocaust.

Yet the Israel that took its actual and political and moral shape after 1967 was impossible to accept. There was nothing empty about the land that had been conquered in 1967, and so it became obvious, as if it were a sudden discovery of modern history, that there was nothing empty about all the land that had been taken for the people without land. Yet some cataclysmic end to Israel was also impossible – it could be imagined but must be prevented. The middle ground between these two extremes, between the two points that defined a spectrum of possible resolutions of the opposites, became a series of peace initiatives, compromises, plans for an end to the repeated eruptions of war. But the possible points of apparent reason along the spectrum tended to fall foul of the defining points at each end.

Here was the terrible contradiction by which so many Jews have been tormented. Many of us became more and more troubled by the tension, more and more alarmed by the slide towards ever greater violence, more and more inclined to be inarticulate, silent. Discussions about Israel became hard to bear; Israel did not represent Judaism, and secular Judaism needed to define itself in political and moral independence from Israel. Yet the horror of the Second World War again cast its long shadows. We found ourselves shifting towards a new form of silence.

Just six years after the Six Day War, in 1973, on the first day of Yom Kippur and the tenth day of Ramadan, the most important and serious of the Jewish and Muslim festivals, Egypt and Syria invaded Israel. I was living in London, and heard a bulletin announcing the invasion on the early morning news. The first reports spoke of an immense military: 100,000 Egyptian soldiers with more than 3,000 tanks and heavy guns crossing the Suez Canal, storming the Israeli defences and military posts. At the same time, 3,000

Syrian troops supported by 150 tanks and 100 planes carrying out bombing raids had attacked Israeli positions on the Golan Heights. Egypt had large numbers of SAM anti-aircraft missile batteries, supplied by the Soviet Union, making it impossible for Israel to repeat the domination of the air that had given it such a rapid victory in 1967. This was a surprise challenge to Israel's occupation of Sinai and Golan; the fight-back against the humiliation inflicted on the Arab world by the Six Day War. A redressing of imbalances, the media were saying. Another war had begun that might determine the political shape of the Middle East, and the destiny of the Jewish state.

Later on that first day of the Yom Kippur War I phoned my parents in Sheffield. My mother answered. She was very anxious; she hated this return to war. There needs to be some success on the Arab side, I said, some way in which this will push Israel into a peace settlement, a return to the pre-1967 borders.

'Don't say these things over the telephone,' said my mother. Over the telephone? What did she mean? 'People will hear you,' she said. At first I was perplexed. Was this her fear of discovery by some anxious image she had of the outside world? However uneasy we might be about Israel's politics, was this something between ourselves, a secret from all others? I asked her what she meant, but all she could say was the same thing, in different forms: whatever you think, do not say it.

———————

One day, in the summer of 1989, my mother and I were alone in the long low sitting room of my home in Cumbria. I had been putting together a family tree – a result of some writing I was doing, and the writing itself a result or concomitant of unhappiness. It was a difficult time; life with the mother of my first two children had failed; I dreaded the changes to come and felt a panic-stricken fear that I would soon not be living with my children. My mother knew I was in the grip of these fears – she was at her best when looked to for real, urgent support. It may be that this unhappiness of mine, the sense that I would have to move out of my home, touched her to the depths of her own experience. Grief summons grief. And grief, for her, was all to do with history. My writing had taken me to a part of this history, to the idea of a family tree: branches that grew, leaves that matured and fell, roots that were invisible, dark and infinite. So I had drawn a simple chart; wanting to fill in the many gaps, I showed it to her. She helped: names came to her without difficulty, and soon there were the cousins, aunts, uncles, grandparents, even second cousins, written into their places on the branches of the tree.

When this was done, she stood looking at it. We were standing alongside the piano; I had laid out the sheets of paper on its music stand. She was silent, reading the names. Then she began to point and say, at each of the names she indicated, 'She perished' or 'He perished'. Just those two words, spoken with a matter-of-factness that was a part of her character. A basic indication of what had happened to her family, the people she had been brought up with and, I knew, had loved with great intensity and had at times missed terribly. I found myself puzzling over the word she chose: 'perished'. Everyone dies; most of those she pointed to would have been dead long since. But to perish is to be gone in an absolute, irrecoverable way – a death that resists the possibility of a memory or a story. A disengagement from the event; or a way of making the event both inevitable and unacceptable. They all perished.

95

In fact, of course, they were all murdered. And in horrifying circumstances. Some in places and ways that were known only in a general sense. To perish at Auschwitz is to die in a way we know about from accounts of others; not from anything victims in our family could tell us, or memories of those who knew them at the time, or eyewitnesses of a particular death. To be 'murdered by the Russians' (as was the case with some of the family my mother spent her summers with, on their estate in southern Poland) was also a particular that, when thought about, becomes vague and uncertain. There was no story of what happened. Perhaps it was even a supposition: they disappeared when the Russians occupied their land, took over their house: so they must have been murdered by the Russians.

Bits of stories, and the absence of stories, came later. That day in Cumbria it was staccato and to the point: they perished. There they stood, on a sheet of paper, at their places on the branches, leaves that had fallen from a family tree. I thought of my mother and grandmother living in England, as the murders took place – in those years of the war – making their new lives for themselves as survivors. I stared at the names, the spread of all that was lost. I remembered my grandmother, soon after the end of the war, in her bed-sitting-room in our house in a Sheffield suburb. Looking at the family tree with its mark alongside each person who had been murdered, I saw that she had lost her father, mother, both her sisters, her brother-in-law and almost all of her husband's family. My mother had shown me some of the details of the devastation and so had implied the anguish that she had had to find a way to live with. She had explained, without having to explain it, why a determination not to pass on such realities to her own children had been part of her choice.

It was no coincidence that this family tree was made at that time. The transformations of 1989 and 1990 – the huge surprises of that moment in history – are already hard to invoke. The Soviet system had yielded, cracked and was about to break in a rush of convulsive events, in the Soviet Union and across all its satellites. Poland had declared itself free of Soviet rule. The Berlin Wall was torn apart; the old, pre-war Germany was taking its former shape. The Cold War was ending. This meant that the real, the hot wars, of the twentieth century, with Germany at the epicentre, had reached their conclusions. The immense global battle that began in 1914 and, it can be said, lasted with periodic lulls into deceptive and short-lived pauses in hostilities, through the 1930s, the Second World War, Korea, Vietnam, the surrogate wars between East and West – this came to an end with the collapse of the Soviet Union, the fall of the Berlin Wall. Divides crumbling; people pouring across the divides; hope. So my mother, standing alongside the piano in an old house deep in the English countryside, began to speak with the new apparent freedom – though this may be the wrong word: not a freedom, since she had always felt free to speak; rather, some subliminal sense that there were no longer any risks to her, nothing to fear. The enemies at last had faded away, had perished – at least for my mother. Perhaps this was the end of history, as history had been for her.

My father the doctor died of emphysema – his lifetime of heavy smoking had wrecked his lungs. He spent the last years, in his seventies, gasping for breath. By that time my parents had moved to a bungalow at the edge of the city, close to the hills where they had always loved to walk. The bungalow was small but elegant – and even now, after a lifetime in England, surprisingly un-English. This was displayed by choices of furniture, paintings, china and glass, some of which my grandmother had managed to bring from Vienna as she fled. My father's lungs at last gave out ten years after they created this new home. My mother was to live there on her own for another twenty-five years.

After my father's death I would make visits to the bungalow, and for the first time in my life, in the aftermath of the fall of the Berlin Wall and the making of the family tree, I sat alone with my mother and asked questions. Questions about her childhood, the escape from Vienna, her relationship with her mother, people she had known, what it had been like to be in England, in Sheffield.

Several times, in different ways, hoping to get below the surface, I said: but you were not always happy, were you? And you had to have your mother with you? And she was not easy, not even liking you, as I remember? And the rows and arguments with her? Didn't you want something else, something more? It must have been very difficult . . . And why did Dad never speak to us? Did he speak to you? Sometimes she began an answer, then hesitated. There were bits of the story she liked to tell, but I wanted to get beyond these. Again and again she would fall back on those old answers: 'I was safe here, that's everything that I can say. What else is there to remember?' 'Your father loved me; that was all I needed.' 'We wanted the best for you boys.'

In fragments from different visits some pieces of her life were touched on. There had been an escape. From the Nazis, but also from the grim coldness of her childhood. Her mother had been a terrible difficulty. Sheffield and its Jewish community had in many ways been awful for her – so few people understood where she came from, who she was; even some relatives made it obvious enough they did not like her. No one had wanted her Hyman to marry her. She was criticised. She felt she could never get anything quite right. And, most difficult of all, she had a husband who loved her but could not talk to her about feelings. He would do all he could to help, in practical ways, but she was alone with grief. And, as she got this far in answering my questions, she always began to cry. Always.

With the tears came words of self-protection and of closure. 'Why do you ask me these questions? What is it you want to know? Why can't you put an arm round me and say well done? I did all I could do. Why do you make me feel we got everything wrong?' Again and again our conversations were halted by this apparent fear, this protective burst of self-pity. No, no, I said. I do not have any criticism in mind. I am full of admiration for the way you made a life. Still, when I think back to childhood, or even when I look at the lives of my children, I see a line of grief that runs through us all, and I want to know where this comes from. Perhaps we can understand . . .

Once, at the close of one of our conversations, she sat in her chair, the *Guardian* crossword puzzle on a small table beside her, looking out at the rose-bed she had created at the front of her wonderful English garden, and she suddenly said, by way of a single answer to all that was implied in my questions: 'I needed to belong; I had never belonged anywhere.' But in Vienna? 'I had school-friends, but I was alone.' The only child with the angry mother; Jewish but assimilated; not assimilated enough to be at ease with being Jewish. Then Sheffield. 'I know I was here on sufferance,' she said. Even in the family? 'My in-laws didn't really welcome me; I was not good enough for your father.'

But you came from such a good family, had so much education. 'And you think they wanted those things? They criticised every decision – I was wrong to let you go skiing, wrong to send you to boarding school.' She looked around the room, at the fine things she had collected and arranged there. At the quiet elegance of her home. This home that was unlike any other on those streets that led past Sheffield to the first farms and the hills. Not better, not richer, but different, foreign, beautiful in its way, hers.

The Jewish community had meant so much to us as children, so we imagined that it was of intense importance to the family. But I wondered, through my questions, what being Jewish had come to mean for her. She had no belief, no ritual she followed, no role in the synagogue, no children or grandchildren who lived Jewish lives, and she had long been troubled by the political morality of Zionism. I asked her if she had thought of going to live in Palestine, rather than travel to England or – as part of her mother's long-term plan for her – go to India. No, no. There was no thought of that. Perhaps they had not been Jewish enough, in Vienna; then, once there was a home in England and children, it never came up. But how was that possible, in the post-war era, as the new state of Israel was being created and Zionism was making its appeal to all Jews to make the *Aliya*, the 'going upwards', as they termed Jewish migration to the Jewish state? No, no, it was not for them; it was for the young, people without a profession, people for whom life had not yet begun. Did they even talk about it? Was Dad interested in the idea? 'No, perhaps he was too Jewish.' I smiled with her at the dichotomy that explained not going there – she not enough, he too much. Zionism had not been part of her heritage, shaped as it was by assimilation and privilege, while the deeply orthodox home of my father's background was far removed from ideals of farm work and nation-building. But Australia – that was where she had wanted to go! In the early years of their marriage, my mother told me, she had urged again and again that they go there. Her favourite neighbours from Vienna, the household where she had always felt most welcome – they had escaped to Sydney at the very beginning of the war. She wanted to join them, she said, and be made welcome again, in the way that she would not feel welcome anywhere else. Australia, not Israel.

In one of our conversations about Judaism and Israel, my mother revealed that she had always felt uneasy in the synagogue. She went there on the main holidays – Passover, Yom Kippur and the New Year, Rosh Hashanah. But, she said, she did this for her husband, the pride she took in his reputation, his standing in that community of Sheffield Judaism. Not for herself. When he died, she would not go there. For a while she joined a rival Jewish community, centred on a Reform rabbi, a repudiation of the old conservatism and orthodoxy. A community where women could be alongside their husbands, and where the English translation of prayers was part of their meaning. But she soon lost interest in that too. 'So did you resign from all membership of the Jewish community?' I asked her. 'I couldn't do that,' she said. 'I want to be buried with your father. My grave must be with his. So I kept paying the membership. If you aren't a member you can't be buried in the Jewish cemetery.' The place where she was sure she did belong was a community of two.

TO START AGAIN

The lines and influences, of history and family, that led me to Israel are only part of my childhood. Other forces – more my own than from my heritage, if that is a distinction that can be held on to – were at work. Birds, fishing, countryside – these turned out to be the foundations for a chance to begin again.

England was where my parents and grandmother found their safety. It was the country that had saved their lives, but where I was never sure who I was, or where I belonged and did not belong. The stories of life were undercut by many echoes of death and loss. The countryside, the outside, brambles in a churchyard or hills and trout streams in Derbyshire – there was an England that I had a sense of belonging to, or where I could go to be and do things that were joyful. But the society that was England, with its constant challenges about who I was or what right I might have to be there, came more and more to make me falter and be unsure. And the stories I had heard about Vienna, the glimpses of the camps I was given at the edge of sleep, the problem of being a Jew while being urged not to be a Jew – all that lay behind being in England had planted seeds of despair. Already, even as a child, I knew that I would find a way to leave this place. Make an escape. To go to Israel was both an attempt to leave and to remain, at least in relation to the family, a way of going but staying within the contradictions by which I was surrounded and, often, confounded.

My first experience of movies was being taken by my mother to a double bill: *Bambi* and *Scott of the Antarctic*. I would have been five or six. The combination of extreme sentimentality and tragic heroism, hope emerging in defiance of difficulty, must have echoed both in the mind of the child and with that moment in British history, and must have done its bit to shape both. This cinema experience also established a connection between great adventure and snowstorms. But the film I remember, which would have been a silent short to go with a feature, was something that made a much more direct appeal. It transported me, for the first time, to Canada.

A fisherman steps into the shallows of a fast-flowing river. He wades into the water, up to his knees, up to his waist. He is wearing shorts and a light shirt. He is looking hard into the clear cold water that glides around boulders, and around him as he stands there. Behind the fisherman there is a steep bank, dense with pine trees. He casts out a line, his eyes focused on the middle of the river. His rod lurches; it bends into a curve. The line begins to stream off its reel. He has hooked a large fish, which swims away from him, fast, downstream. The force of the water is giving the fish great strength. The fisherman begins to wade down through the water, the current piling against him. Then, to my amazement, he half falls, half dives into the water and lets the current sweep him along. With one arm he holds the rod as high as he can above the surface; with the other he swims and steers himself around the boulders. He is carried towards faster water, and on into foaming rapids. Still he holds up the rod and does his best to swim. His head and arm up, the rod above him, he is swirling through the rapids, until he comes to a calmer pool below and is able to swim towards the shore, into the shallows and clamber out onto the riverbank. He walks downstream, along the river's edge, still doing battle. At last the fish is too tired to struggle: floundering on the surface, it is brought to the shore. The fisherman tugs it onto a gravel bar, lays down his rod and pulls the fish beyond the water's edge. He lifts it up: a huge salmon. Standing there at the side of a great river, the forested banks all around him, water dripping from him, he is laughing with delight. This was Canada.

A few years later, as a young teenager, on another trip to the countryside with my friend Alex's family, I met a Canadian. He told us he was from Nova Scotia. I had never heard of it, but I asked if there was good fishing there. His answer was a shower of enthusiasm. He described the rivers, talked of the forests they flowed through. I asked who the rivers and the fishing belonged to – this had already become a problem: most of the places I wanted to go and fish were private, ring-fenced with the privilege or exorbitant daily charges of the landed gentry.

Then the man from Nova Scotia gave the astonishing facts: no one owned the rivers or the fishing, anyone could fish there. Anyone? Anyone who would buy a licence. You didn't have to be invited? And what did it cost? Questions jumped out of our amazement. We must be sure to come and visit, he said. He would take us out to catch salmon, many salmon. Shooting too – for ducks and deer. In a vast, wild, forested, free terrain. A set of terrains. A whole universe of space and freedom. Canada became a place to believe in.

The Canadian talked about salmon and elk, water and forests, not about society. Yet his words let me glimpse a possibility of freedom that was impossible in the England I was growing up in. It was somewhere that had nothing to do with being or not being a Jew. A place far away from those images of death. I imagined that in Canada the air would be clean and cold and easy to breathe. A different sort of promised land. Caught in the class-ridden countryside, on the class-shaped pheasant shoots, I was both finding myself and beginning to see ways to escape. I was meeting and attempting to deal with the forces for which I still had no language but from which I was managing to discern an alternative, a version of elsewhere.

Israel was to be a first attempt at getting far away, but it took me back into the depths of where I came from, the shadows of European history, the dreadful, revelatory words my grandmother had murmured to me. After Israel came university, a job teaching philosophy and then the realisation, at last, that I should become an anthropologist.

This was the profession of other places. With the help of scholarships, field work in the west of Ireland, supportive teachers and friends, I made the initial journeys, and wrote the first pieces about what going to other ways of being could reveal. But I needed to travel farther, away from any piece of Europe. I read more and more about societies far removed from the European agricultural traditions; I found descriptions of hunter-gatherers. And it was not long before I began to think of the far north as the most compelling place to be an anthropologist – in the very far north of Canada, on the margins of the inhabitable world, beyond the reach of farms or even roads, remote from anywhere I had ever been.

There, among people who were hunters and gatherers, I would have to learn everything – a language unlike any other I had been taught, a way of being in the world that would be unfamiliar, and a life that was set deep within the land. The anthropologist who learns through immersion in another society becomes the child. It is a chance, which has to be taken, to start again.

AND THE NORTH

I went to the Arctic for the first time in 1970. First to the Inuktitut language school in Rankin Inlet, then to Pond Inlet, at the north end of Baffin Island. I flew north in the Arctic early spring. The houses of Rankin were still half buried in snow and, at the shore below the houses, the sea-ice stretched off into the distance. The first day I arrived I walked out onto the rim of the ice, finding a way among the heaped boulder-like chunks of ice that had been frozen onto the beach. I was full of trepidation, afraid that I was about to be attacked by a polar bear and unsure if I would ever be able to manage this astounding, utterly unfamiliar place. I remember thinking that this was the first time I had ever felt completely free of the allergies and asthma that had plagued my childhood. And free in my soul because I was so far from anything I knew. My job was to learn – the language, the way of life, the challenges, the complications of change. I was to spend many months living and travelling with Inuit families.

In Pond Inlet I stayed with the family of Inuk and Inujak, a warm and easy-going middle-aged couple whose house was in the middle of the settlement. Whenever possible, however, often at the urging of my Inuktitut teachers, I went out onto the land, to be with hunters, travelling by both dog-team and snowmobile. I have many times struggled to find the words with which to share the beauty of that land and the joy of being shown what it was, and what it means, to the people of the north.

The light, the way the sun circled in the sky all through the spring and summer; the winter, when for many weeks the darkness yielded only for a short spell of midday twilight. The cold, when all moisture in the air became tiny ice crystals, and every breath could cause frost to build up on the fur trim of a parka and on any unshaved part of my face. The heat, when the miracle of caribou-skin clothing meant that my body was so well insulated that I would have to flap the wind through my jacket to cool down. The ice in so many forms and shapes – great blocks and ridges of frozen sea that had been forced up onto the shoreline at the beginning of winter; the vast spread of the frozen surface of the sea itself, and icebergs locked into it and then drifting across the horizon through the summer. And the snow – fresh falling, driven in the wind, packed tight on top of the sea-ice, melted and refrozen – I was able to learn some of the words Inuit used to speak of its many forms. Every part of this world astonished me for its scale – immensity of landscape, many thousands of square miles that were the home and territories of the hunters, journeys of days, sometimes weeks, across the ice, along fjords, over the tundra, across the mountains. And the unbelievable beauty.

So far removed, out at the extremes and edges of my world, often bewildering, at times frightening, yet I felt at home, in the depths of my being. Some of this came from links that did exist between the far north and the places I had lived before. There were birds that I knew, or had read about in my great childhood bird book; nests and eggs I had found as text and paintings. Now I was thrilled at seeing, for real, king eiders, rock ptarmigan, falcons and long-tailed skuas. When the Inuit realised that this was a special enthusiasm of mine they made a point of teaching me all the names they had for birds, and all the uses they made of them. In one community, they even created a collection of eggs they found when out on hunting trips. I made a study of the alpine plants too – another surprising reminder of home, the rockery in the garden in Sheffield.

But the deep ease I felt being there came from the welcome I was given, both out on the land and in the houses of the settlements: the warmth, generosity and humour of everyday life. It took me some time to understand that this welcome, and the ease I was made to feel, came from qualities of personality and society that were deeply embedded in Inuit hunter-gatherer ways of being on their land and with one another. A flood of both anthropology and delight. This was indeed a homecoming, the chance to begin again.

Within a few weeks of arriving in Pond Inlet, like all southerners who spent any length of time in the Arctic, I had been given an Inuktitut name. Mirqukuluk. *Mirqu* is the word for body hair. The suffix *-kuluk* translates very much as the Scottish word 'wee', implying a mixture of being small and nice. The wee hairy one. After I had been working in the north for about a year, Anaviapik had begun to call me *Irninguaq*, adoptive son, and told me that I should know his wife, Ulajuk, as *Anannanguaq*, adoptive mother. When we were out on the land, Anaviapik would call me by names that referred to what we were doing together – *Qimmuksiqatik*, dog-team partner, for example, or, more generally, *Piqatik*, the person he was with.

Older Inuit were always uneasy about using someone's real name. At birth everyone was given a name that came from a much loved relative, often someone who had died not long before the birth of the person being given the name. In the same way, the name of the elder who had died also came from a close relative

of theirs. Thus names reached back into the timeless past. To give a name was to bring the ancestor back to the world, as a form of reincarnation. So to speak a name out loud was to risk association with the spirit world of the ancestors. The use of words to establish kinship and actual shared activity was to hold others in the web of connections. Thus when I was given these names I too was drawn into the community, given a place, as a newborn, in that system. Nothing could have been more welcome to me. For all that I was the extreme outsider, I was given to understand in this way that I belonged. And, once I was given this sense of belonging, I felt able to ask those who had thus adopted me to share their stories.

The community that I was welcomed into was small – no more than 500 people lived at the north tip of Baffin Island. Over the three years that I spent time there I came to know just about every family, and visited most homes many times. But the land that they travelled, and knew in extraordinary detail, was immense. After working in the Arctic for three years, I became one of a team that had the job of mapping Inuit relationships to their environment. The Canadian government had agreed to negotiate indigenous claims to their lands, and the Inuit were among the very first to look for a way to make these claims visible. Maps were a device for achieving this.

From the very beginning I was uneasy about it being called a 'claim' – after all, it is colonists and settlers who lay claim to the lands of others. Nonetheless, this was a chance for the Inuit to establish beyond any doubt or question that the Arctic was indeed theirs. Prior to this mapping work, the Inuit had never spoken to me in terms of 'owning' their land – rather, it was the setting in which they lived, hunted, travelled, and, as the elders kept pointing out to me, this land was given its life by their knowledge.

So the mapping may have changed forever the way that the land was seen, by both the Inuit and government: it now became a contested zone, an arena of possession and, therefore, potential dispossession. I had the job of building with the people the maps that would show their rights to the eastern high Arctic, with all the places that I had been taken to by dog-team, skidoo and innumerable stories.

I knew it was a large area; when I came to put the topographical sheets together, I discovered that we would have to map onto a base that extended over 450 miles from east to west, and 400 miles from north to south. This large area was made all the more extensive by its fractured topography: the multitude of bays, inlets, islands and mountains meant that those who used this land travelled along routes that twisted and turned, headed out across spans of open water and far inland along dramatic fjords and long river valleys. I knew that many families had often travelled to hunt or visit with relatives and neighbouring settlements that were 150 miles away; one family I knew had made an extended journey of over a thousand miles, moving from one Inuit community to another, all the way to the tree line, far to the southwest. Putting together all the map sheets for this extent of land use meant making a set of base maps that was five feet across.

In house after house, people squatted and crouched around this great area of virtual territory. We went through the list. Mark all the places you have hunted for ring seal, bearded seal, harp seal, walrus, narwhal . . . And the places you hunted for caribou, hare, polar bears . . . And trapped foxes . . . And fished for Arctic char, trout, cod, sculpin . . . And gathered mussels, sea urchins . . . And hunted eider ducks, snow geese, tundra swans . . . And collected the eggs of Arctic terns, murres, gulls, black guillemots . . . And picked blueberries, cranberries . . . Show all this for when you were living out on the land before the school was set up. Now all the places since the school. And where were the graves of your ancestors, the campsites you used, the places you put your tents? Then the ecological knowledge: the bears' dens; the way cracks formed in the ice in spring and meant that seals and narwhal could be hunted in the open water; which way the caribou moved in spring and autumn; where they had their calves; where their favourite summer grazing was. Someone mentioned spiders – were there many in this particular place? And butterflies. Someone had picked mushrooms – where were they usually found? And journeys – to trade one year, to visit a sick relative another, to travel for the fun of travelling. Along this shoreline, across that mountain pass, then down the coastline there. These were the places we stopped. Here there was a bad storm, and across that headland the ice was always piled high in early spring so it was slow and difficult to use that route . . . And here is where you can find the bones of my grandparents, and here is the grave of a southerner who came there to trade, and the wreck of an old whaling ship . . .

One map biography could take two days, and then be added to during extra visits, more stories, another layer of memories. We worked and worked, all of every day, for weeks on end. The maps became filled with circles, lines, notes, and the maps piled up. Everyone was able to find themselves on these maps. They could see their world in these representations from above, as with a bird's eye view, which they could never have had; it was as easy for them as any other, more usual way of seeing their lands. The laying out of all this experience and knowledge was to reveal what it had meant to be a hunter and gatherer in these territories. For all their clutter of information, crossings out and corrections, lines going in all directions in many different colours, the maps were compelling and beautiful creations. They showed just how intense, extensive and rich the Inuit relationship to their world had been, and still was.

They showed this to me, the outsider who had brought this inquiry into their homes. They also showed it to one another. No one did their mapping in solitude; members of the family sat and watched, neighbours who were visiting joined in. This was work that celebrated Inuit experience and skill. Everyone was delighted to show, tell, share. Everyone took pride in what was being revealed. They also found a new appreciation for their system: a pattern of land use and harvests that depended on extended family groups. Each group had its set of hunting, fishing, trapping and living sites. Inuit life depended on a seasonal round, with winter seal hunting areas out on the sea-ice where a number of households would gather; then a spreading out to spring hunting places; a further scatter to summer caribou hunting inland or coastal hunting where kayaks and skin boats could be used; then a move to autumn fishing places at a river where the char were migrating upstream; and back to the winter seal hunting. Each group had a set of such places. In winter some groups might overlap; for much of the year each group would move among its particular series of living sites and territories, along its distinctive seasonal round. As we made the maps, the shapes of these seasonal movements emerged – everyone could see that between them they had created a large and widespread system of interconnected patterns of hunting, fishing, gathering and trapping. Each family spoke only for its particular part of the large pattern, but to see it as a whole was to understand the brilliance and completeness of Inuit use of their lands and their stories about their lives. When all the maps were put together, every possible harvesting area and living site had been used; everywhere and everything was known and understood. Stories became maps; maps turned into a new kind of story.

I never thought to myself that this was the way I had needed my family in England to share their history, to pass on their stories. At the time I was not aware of how vital the building of memory is for wellbeing, but I would feel surges of energy, of strange happiness, as I was taken into the sophistication of the hunting life and this immense encyclopaedia of Inuit knowledge.

Not just knowledge, not only an array of facts, but also a way of having and sharing what is in the mind. The telling of stories, the sharing of memories, the drawing of others into a circle of knowledge, all that is achieved in oral culture – these too showed me what it can mean to be an adult in relation to the natural world, alive to the environment in order to be alive in all ways. This made every kind of sense to me. Through this discovery of Inuit ways of knowing, teaching and learning, I was learning about their complex of achievements and discovering a good deal about what it meant to be a coherent human being. They were parents to me; I grew up under their tutelage to a realisation of what it can mean to be human. I was being shown that the version of human nature I had been urged to accept by my anxious parents and the justifications of greed and the market economy offered by European philosophers was neither natural nor inevitable.

———————

At night, in a snow house or tent, I listened to the sounds of the north. In spring the quack-like calls of ptarmigan; in winter the hiss of a naphtha-fuelled stove; at every season the voices of the storytellers. Again and again I lay, almost asleep, as someone was describing a hunt, sometimes going over the events of the last days, bringing to mind some detail that was surprising or funny, sometimes remembering another time or place, taking us to mythic adventures. Speaking as they always spoke. In the quiet of the end of day, in the warmth of a one-room home, there was no question of silence – other than to pause between stories.

One family that often took me with them on hunting trips among a group of islands in southern Hudson Bay liked to end the day with ghost stories. We lay in a line, each sleeping bag right up against the next, and drifted off to sleep while someone told of an encounter with the supernatural. They had such skills as storytellers, playful and witty – seeing if they could make us shout out in surprise or feel a shiver of fear. Sometimes as we lay there, they would call on me to tell a story or answer a question. Once, as we lay in our sleeping bags, a young hunter asked me why it was that the southerners, white people, the Qallunaat, were always thinking about money. In his land, he said, if you were hungry or needed something, your neighbours would feed you or help you, but you didn't ask for money. So here in the north, the most important things in life could work well without any thought of money. But, he went on, he understood that everything you needed, when living in the south, in the land of the Qallunaat, had a price. It was my turn to tell a story – about how people lived in the world I had come from. I tried to use what I had learned of this new language to talk about the old things, from far away, but I stumbled, became incoherent, and fell back on a ghost story.

I lay in a tent, with the light of a candle and the warmth of a simple stove, with a family who shared everything with me because they shared everything with one another, far out on the land that was so much at the centre of its world.

Places where everything was bought and sold seemed too far away to think about. Yet they were, in political reality, not so very distant. The young man who asked me the question about money knew that everything was changing, and that the life in the family tent was at risk. Speaking in their own language, in their own homes or, best of all, out on their lands, the people I lived and travelled with were in no way silenced. Yet the new forces, already at work in their settlements and minds, threatened to stifle their voices, to be the cause of a new silence. Many Inuit, both elders and youth, said to me, in different ways but with considerable resolve, that they needed to confront the forces working against them, but theirs was a culture where confrontation should almost always be avoided. If they did overcome the reluctance to confront, they faced the problem of language – they needed to be understood, but many of those they most wanted to be understood by had to be spoken to in English. And those they needed to speak to had all the power – that alone could be a reason for keeping quiet.

I learned that there was a word in Inuktitut for this kind of fear – *ilira*. This was the feeling that those with frightening and unfathomable powers inspired in those they dominate. Ghosts caused you to feel *ilira*; so did the police constables and government officials from the south.

After I had known him for almost two years, Anaviapik, my mentor and, he liked to say, my adoptive father in the north, once said to me, 'If we Inuit said what we really think, if we spoke out against the government and the oil companies that are taking over our land, they would very quickly come and kill us.' As he said this he made a gathering gesture with his arms, to suggest a corralling of his people, then turned to another elder who was sitting with us, saying, 'Isn't that what you think?' 'Yes,' she said. 'That's what we think they would do, that's the danger.'

I was to learn that the Arctic had already been suffering from various forms of abuse – of the people and their land. The damage caused by colonial aims, and the behaviour of the representatives of colonialism, became the core of my ten years of work in the Canadian north. A series of episodes, in the course of that work and more recently when I returned to Pond Inlet after forty years of absence, kept leading me back to the strengths of Inuit heritage, which had taught me so much about the world and, with its adoption of me into the everyday life of the Arctic, had filled a void in my own life. Yet, at the same time, I became more and more disturbed by the layers of accumulating abuse and the deep damage done. Many of the consequences of this neither they nor I had been able to face while I was living there.

─────────

The Rankin Inlet language school had been set up for the Canadian government by the charismatic linguist and teacher Mick Mallon. It was there in 1970 that I met Don McCoy. Don was the Settlement Manager of the only government settlement on the Belchers, a group of islands some ninety miles from the Hudson Bay coast of Arctic Quebec. Settlement Managers were the government representatives assigned at that time to each community in what was then the Northwest Territories of Canada. Don, like all Settlement Managers in the eastern Arctic, had been encouraged to take the Mallon course to help him do his job better. I was there because I had a contract from a research group within the Canadian Department of Indian and Northern Affairs. My job, they told me, was to spend at least a year in the Arctic learning Inuktitut and that I should begin by taking the Mick Mallon course. Don and I were fellow newcomers to Inuktitut but he had already been in the north for several months. He told me about the Belchers.

Inuit called it Qikiqtait. *Qikiqtaq* is Inuktitut for an island; *-it* at the end, replacing the last sound of the word, makes it plural. The *Qikiqtarmiut* are 'people of the islands', Inuit who have lived for many generations on Qikiqtait. In the 1960s the Canadian federal government established a single permanent settlement on those islands. The Inuit named this settlement Sanikiluaq, in honour of an elder who had been famous for his prodigious skills as a hunter and, most of all, for his ability to run long distances with extraordinary speed.

Government settlements were clusters of houses and southern outposts – police stations, churches, schools and trading posts – that the government had decided should be the permanent homes and service centres for the many families that, until that time, had lived in a scatter of hunting and trapping camps throughout the Arctic. These settlements were the result of a post-war policy to incorporate all of the country, even its remotest edges, into the Canadian nation; they came with a new conviction that the far north had vast economic potential.

Don invited me to come and spend some time in the settlement on the Belcher Islands. One of the very last places in the Arctic to be discovered by Europeans, isolated off the Quebec shore of Hudson Bay, southern institutions had only just begun to be set up on the islands. Don told me that there was no police station, no missionary and just a small nursing station. The Hudson's Bay

Company had run a trading post there since the 1930s, and there had been a small primary school since the late 1960s. Although life was now based on the new government settlement, this looked to be an Inuit world where language, culture and links to the land continued to be very strong. I was already expected at Pond Inlet, but resolved to visit the Belchers as soon as possible.

After several months in Pond Inlet, I suggested to Christine, my girlfriend back in London, that she come for a visit to the north and that we go together to the Belchers. I got in touch with Don, accepted his invitation, and in mid-August set off from Pond Inlet to Sanikiluaq. This meant flying all the way south to Montreal, where I met Christine, and from there up to Great Whale River, the jumping-off point for the islands off the coast of Arctic Quebec. There were no scheduled flights or boats beyond Great Whale River. We had to wait until there was some way of getting across the ninety miles of sea that separated Qikiqtait from the mainland. After a delay of two or three days, we hitched a ride on a small float plane that was taking some building supplies out to Sanikiluaq.

At the end of a short but nerve-wracking, bumpy ride the plane, from which we had looked down in amazement at the tangle of islands and rocky islets that composed the Belchers, landed in the bay in front of the settlement – two short rows of houses along a low-lying shore. A gravel beach made it possible to pull up canoes – and disembark from float planes. Don and a large group of Inuit met the plane, helped us ashore and made us welcome. Don took us up to the large and well-equipped house built for the Settlement Manager. We stayed with him there for about a week.

Then the Inuit we had met, including the Qittisuk and Aragutainaq families, offered us the use of a small shack at the north-west end of the community, which had for a time been a tiny museum, created some five years before as the community's way of celebrating the centenary of Canada's creation in 1867. Some remarkable items of Qikiqtarmiut material culture were still being stored there. We found ourselves living in a place that had a wonderful reek of the past and, perhaps most important, was very much like the housing Inuit had built for themselves, when first able to get hold of southern building materials. Small shacks put together with rough timber and tarred felt became the norm in many seasonal camps and at the places where traders and missionaries began to build their posts and churches. Just like those first modern Inuit homes, we had a basic oil stove, a large aluminium barrel to hold water, and not much else. We created a sleeping area at one end of the space, and improvised some bits of furniture to set up a kitchen and living area at the other. There was a small lean-to that had been added to one side of the building, which was where we put the 'honey bucket', as the minimal form of toilet was called.

The significance of this museum turned into a shack to live in was very great: we set up a home where elders, and indeed everyone, were happy to visit. Our museum-shack was reminiscent of Inuit life at the very margins of, or beyond, most southern influences. This was reinforced by the rather basic conditions in which we lived – everything was more or less as the Inuit were accustomed to and liked: the informality that came with an absence of armchairs, pieces of seal and freshly killed ducks in the entrance way, eating pots of boiled meat sitting on the floor, and, thanks to Christine, a regular flow of fresh baked bread. I suspect that even the dearth of washing facilities added to the feeling of comfort. This was not an environment in which southerners were setting up customs or expectations that were new and potentially oppressive. We had not come with any ideas about what people should or should not do, think, eat or believe; rather we were there to live more or less as the least 'modernised' of Sanikiluaq were living.

For all that I have written about my work with and for Inuit, I have written very little about Sanikiluaq. Something constrained me, though it is hard to understand quite what this was. My time there was rich with many experiences both out on the land and when living in the settlement; the people were always welcoming and eager to help me understand their language and their world. The beauty of those islands and of the people for whom this was their home were clear to me then, and are so now as I bring them to mind. But there is a thread of darkness running through these memories, intimations embedded in the stories the people of Sanikiluaq shared with me that were perplexing and difficult but, I am sure, of vital importance. There was also a shocking reality that I failed to see. These are stories that raise some of the questions of life and death that have been central to Inuit experience, and are turning out to be of urgent importance for us all.

———

Within a week of arriving in Sanikiluaq Christine and I made friends with the Aragutainaq family. The elders were Noah and Annie. Their older children lived in other houses, with their own families. But Noah's two children by an earlier marriage, Lottie and Joe, and Lottie's adopted baby Apaqanikik, lived with Noah and Annie. As did their youngest daughter Alice, and her husband Peter Kattuk, as well as their adopted son George, and Annie's youngest child Lucassie, then about eighteen years old. All nine of them lived in the three-bedroom house.

Just about every family welcomed us into their homes and lives, and the Aragutainaq household invited us again and again to visit them, to share food, to tell stories. Lucassie became my Sanikiluaq Inuktitut teacher. The whole family offered overwhelming warmth and friendship; a reminder of the way in which Inuit across the north had anticipated and understood what southerners might need, and went to every length to be helpful. I came to feel both great appreciation and deep affection for them. The more time I spent either in their crowded home or out on the land, travelling on sledges and in boats, staying in their tents and cabins, the happier and more at ease I became.

The welcome by the Sanikiluaq community was reinforced about two weeks after arriving there by a message I received from Lucassie Qitisuk, an elderly man who appeared to be the most senior figure in the community. He wanted to meet with me. This rather formal approach filled me with apprehension, but my alarm was wrong-headed. He did ask me why I had come to stay in Sanikiluaq, but told me that he wanted to know because if everyone knew what I needed then they would all be able to help me.

One of Annie Aragutainaq's daughters was married to Jonnie Kavvik, a very active and effective hunter. Along with Noah Aragutainaq and Peter Kattuk, Jonnie often took us out onto the land. Days of hunting would end in a tent set up on the shoreline. Every night, as we all lay there, people would convey an affectionate greeting to one another, as a way of saying goodnight. They did this by adding -ngai to the end of someone's name. The -ngai is a close equivalent to the use, especially in Canada, of 'eh?' Or the French n'est-ce pas? It calls for the answer yes. So, in a tent out on the land, at night, in the heart of the Arctic and the warmth of an Inuit family, I would hear *Hughngai*, and I would reply *Aa*, the 'a' stretched out and soft with an exhaling of breath, *yes*. Then, a minute later, I would respond to whoever had called to me: *Alisingai* or *Lucassingai*, and there would come back to me their *Aa, Aa, yes*.

After I had been on the islands for no more than a few weeks, I was walking along the shoreline below the houses. A middle-aged man was heading towards me, dressed in an old parka that pulled over the head, in the style of the Inuit. Southerners always had parkas with a zip up the front. Yet he looked like a Qallunaaq, a person from the south. I realised that this was someone in Sanikiluaq I had not met. He came up to me to say hello. Shaking my hand and speaking in Inuktitut, he said he had not seen me before, and that he had just returned to Sanikiluaq from a visit to a settlement on the mainland. He said his name was Ali Apaqquq, and that his father was Saumialuk. I did not recognise either of these names, but had yet to get to know all the principal families. Ali was about sixty, taller than many of the Inuit men I had met, and, like almost all Inuit at that time, strongly built. He was very friendly, asked me questions about how I liked Sanikiluaq, where else I had been, how long I might be staying, and urged me to come visit him.

Later that day I mentioned to Alice, a friend in the Aragutainaq family, that I had met Ali Apaqquq. Yes, she said, she had heard from him that he had spoken with me. What did I think of him, she asked. I told her he seemed to be nice, but I was surprised that he looked so much like a Qallunaaq. That's because he takes after his father, she said. That was Saumialuk, which means the big left-hander. I knew from this that Alice was speaking of someone who was not Inuit – only the names given to outsiders, the Qallunaat, are given translations. And she told me that Ali's big left-handed father was Robert Flaherty. He was the first southerner ever to land on the islands, she said, and had stayed there for some time. Long enough to have a son with one of the island women. Alice told me that she had heard that Saumialuk had later lived in other parts of the Arctic, but Ali had never seen him and his southern father had never acknowledged this son of his. Perhaps he did not even know about him. Nevertheless, Ali was proud of having that first white visitor to the islands as his father.

Robert Flaherty is best known for having created *Nanook of the North*, released in 1922, the first and perhaps most influential feature-length documentary film ever made. The footage from which Flaherty edited *Nanook* was almost all shot on the mainland of Arctic Quebec six and seven years after he had lived on the Belchers. In his later years, Flaherty liked to tell the story of his discovery of those islands, which were not to be found on any of the maps or charts of the day, and whose existence was denied even by traders who had lived for many years on that coast. The ninety miles between the islands and Quebec was enough to keep them invisible and unknown to all but the Inuit who lived there. Even though they had often come to trade fox skins for supplies of tea, sugar and tobacco at the posts on the coast, stories they and others told about the islands beyond sight out in Hudson Bay were not believed.

In 1909 the young Flaherty was working for a mining company that aimed to find and develop iron ore deposits in the Ungava peninsula, the huge area of lakes and tundra that stretches across the north-east frontier of Quebec up to the border with

Labrador. Flaherty, who had studied mineralogy, had the job of travelling the land looking for evidence of iron. As part of this endeavour, he decided he should cross the Ungava peninsula by dog-team. The young man he hired to be his guide for this adventure was George Weetaltuk.

Flaherty liked talking with Weetaltuk. They had long evenings together in the tent they shared. He asked him where he came from. Qikiqtait, the islands, said Weetaltuk, but white people don't believe they exist. Flaherty asked him to explain where they were, how far off the coast, and what they were like. Weetaltuk told Flaherty about his people: there were many families, he said, living out there. The Qikiqtarmiut. They were expert at hunting from kayaks, and wore fine, warm clothes made from eider-duck skins. He drew a map for Flaherty to show him the complex swirl of islands and islets that people like Flaherty did not believe in.

This map has become a famous example of the remarkable facility Inuit have shown for representing their lands on paper. The Weetaltuk map, often printed in books about cartography alongside a satellite image of the same islands, is fascinating for its complexity and precision. When Flaherty saw this map he wanted to estimate the length of the longest island, containing, according to Weetaltuk's drawing, an immense lake. George told Flaherty that to make the journey from one end of that island to the other by dog-team would take at least three days. Knowing that Inuit dog-teams travelled about thirty miles per day, Flaherty estimated that this one island must be at least ninety miles long. This, along with much of the detail of shorelines, bays, headlands and outlying islets, turned out to be accurate. Weetaltuk was able to see in his mind's eye, and then transfer to a drawing on a piece of paper a multitude of details of this land where he had once lived. He was able, moreover, to retain the internal proportions, the relative distances between the different elements of his map. He created for Flaherty a precise picture of an archipelago that extended across some 4,500 square miles.

Flaherty was so impressed by this map, so convinced by Weetaltuk's apparent clarity and detail, and so excited by this evocation of a land thus far undiscovered by Europeans, that he resolved to find these islands out in Hudson Bay. His first attempt to reach them was by dog-team, hoping to make a journey that Weetaltuk had told him was possible during the years when the ice in early spring created a solid bridge all the way from Richmond Gulf on the mainland to the south-east shore of the largest of the islands. But the ice in 1910, when Flaherty wanted to make the crossing, was not solid; he had to abandon the attempt. He then decided that the best way to get there would be by boat, sailing in summer out of St John's, Newfoundland, going north up the Labrador coast, and following the shore through Hudson Strait into Hudson Bay. This meant a journey of 200 miles along the Ungava peninsula. Sailing in the *Laddie*, a small but sturdy boat that he found in St John's, Flaherty and a crew of four managed the long route around the coast, and reached the area where the Belchers were supposed to be, only to be caught in thick fog. Navigating with great difficulty, the *Laddie* ran aground. When the fog cleared, he saw that they had indeed been shipwrecked on rocks very close to a large island, and that several kayaks were being paddled by the people of those islands, the Qikiqtarmiut, wearing their eider-duck clothing. Flaherty had found the place and the people that George Weetaltuk had described.

A few days after meeting Ali Apaqquq, I visited him and his family in their three-bedroom government-built house in the two rows of houses that made up the Sanikiluaq community. We sat together in his crowded living room-kitchen, his wife and others in the family gathered around to watch this unfamiliar visitor. Ali and his wife were warm and gracious, expressing their pleasure that I had come to visit. I was in my first months of learning Inuktitut, and had been having some difficulty with the distinctive dialect of the Ungava region – spoken much faster and with many more glottal stops than the north Baffin dialect I had been learning – but we managed a long conversation. Ali, like so many of the Inuit I had spent time with, was quick to assess the Inuktitut vocabulary and grammar I could manage and no doubt took care to speak to me within that level as much as he could.

I can no longer bring to mind all that was said, but I remember him telling me about the house that his father Robert Flaherty, Saumialuk, had built. It was on an island to the south, not far from where many families had lived before being relocated in the Sanikiluaq settlement. Made of boards that they took from their ship, it was a single room with a form of magical lighting. There were pipes of some sort that ended in lanterns. It was heated by an iron wood-stove, which also must have come from the ship. Saumialuk and his crew welcomed Inuit visitors to this house, and were always friendly and generous. They hunted for themselves but also were given meat; in return they gave things to the Inuit that they needed, especially knives. He also told me that after Saumialuk left the islands Inuit had used his cabin when hunting in that area in spring and summer, but then it had burned down – perhaps an accident with the wood-stove, perhaps some moment of puzzling vandalism.

I made journeys with hunters to the south end of the islands, and stayed in at least one of the small one- or two-room houses where Inuit had lived before being pressed into relocating to the

Sanikiluaq settlement. This move had not been welcomed by the families who had been living at what they referred to as South Camp. For them the hunting and fishing was much better here than to the north, and they took deep pleasure in the places that they knew best. They showed me what they said was the best fishing place, the most sheltered camping areas, and were delighted when, during a spring visit, we found the nests of both *savvak*, red-breasted phalarope, and *mitiviarjuk*, the female king eider. I had seen neither of these, they liked to point out, around Sanikiluaq, up there in the north. They told me that all who had been living in the south of the islands were unhappy about the move, which had taken place just five years before, and they did not much like being made to live in the same place as the families whose hunting had always been more up there, in the northern parts of the islands. They were told this was the only way that their children could get an education, and if they refused schooling for their children they would lose other benefits. They were given to understand that this was what all the powerful agencies wanted them to do – the traders, missionaries and police. People had come to rely on southern goods and trading; they were persuaded that schooling for their children was important. But they wanted and needed the changes to leave them able to live in their outposts, where they could be close to a supply of food and a way of life that was theirs. The proposal that they move was backed by veiled threats of force. It was a government demand they thought was wrong. They wanted to say no; they had to say yes.

At night, in the cabin where the Aragutainaq family had last lived before the move, people reminisced about the good times they had known when living here. In the warmth of that family, in the comfort of their cabin, living in a way that pre-dated the government settlements, it felt like another, better era. Those trips to South Camp did not include a side-trip to the place where Flaherty had built his cabin, but people told me more about him. I also learned more about Ali.

———————

One day I came back to Sanikiluaq from a hunting trip to find a note beside a small cassette tape recorder that I used for making spoken notes, learning the language and listening to music. The note was written in Inuktitut syllabics, the script that a Wesleyan missionary first devised in the 1840s for translating parts of the Bible and prayer book into Cree, the language of the First Nation whose lands reached up to James Bay and the Hudson Bay shore, bordering Inuit territories. Inuit across the Canadian central and eastern Arctic had adopted this writing system in the late 1870s and made it their own. At the Inuktitut language school in Rankin Inlet, Mick Mallon had insisted that we learn the basics of this writing system. Then my Inuit teachers in Pond Inlet had insisted that I be able to write it well. Anaviapik had urged this at our very first lesson: he told me that he was sure to become very fond of me but, like all southerners, I would go away again, so I must be able to write to him, and read what he wrote to me.

The note alongside the tape recorder was just a few lines. It was written by Isaac Amituq, an elder I had spent many hours with listening to stories and who had taken me out seal hunting. Isaac told me in these few lines of syllabics that he had recorded something for me. It was about *tammartuvinit*. The root of this word, *tammaq*, has various connotations, all to do with making a mistake or getting something wrong. The word for compass uses the same root, and literally means to prevent losing one's way. The ending, *vinit*, establishes that it happened very much in the past, and carries the implication that the events being referred to were not well understood at the time. So Isaac was telling a story about the mistake makers, those who had unknowingly gone astray. It was his memory of, and his part in, a series of tragic events that engulfed many people of the islands. (I would learn later that these events took place between 1940 and 1942.) Isaac opened his recording by saying that he wanted me to hear this from the tape; it was not a story he wanted to tell in front of others. His account of *tammartuvinit* began.

It was a night in winter. Isaac's family had come to trade, and were camped near the Hudson's Bay Company post, which at that time was at the south end of the islands. They were going to sleep when they heard someone going round and round the outside of their tent, calling out to them. They recognised the voice. It was Peter Sala, a man who had a reputation as a powerful shaman. He was telling them that God was now with them and Jesus was coming.

At that time no missionary had ever stayed on the Belchers, but the influence of missionaries had reached them. A young Inuit man who had spent time with a missionary on the mainland had come back to the islands as an enthusiastic convert, and had with him a copy of sections of the Bible, in Inuktitut, written in syllabics. People were familiar with some of the Bible stories. Isaac described how he lay in his family tent, hearing that God and Jesus were at hand, and wanting to believe it. He was being reminded of the Bible stories, and of the power that the Inuit had heard lay behind them. He went on to talk about the reasons for belief that were not so much to do with the stories but the difficulties that the Inuit were facing that year. Arctic foxes, the crucial item that southern traders wanted to buy, had been hard to find – it was a low point in the extreme fluctuations of the Arctic fox population cycle. Some Inuit, including Sala, had asked for credit to see them through a period of great hardship. The factor at the post had refused them. In desperation, afraid of starvation, needing food and essential supplies – sugar, flour, biscuits, tea and tobacco – to deal with the failure of the hunt and their new reliance on the traders' supplies, as well as ammunition for their hunting rifles, two young Inuit men had attempted to break into the store. The factor had caught them, and beaten one of them severely. Isaac said that some time later he died of what the people said was the result of being hit in the kidneys. Refused credit and too afraid or too respectful of Qallunaaq authority to try again to ransack the Hudson's Bay Company stores, many families were in a dangerous predicament.

Sala, as a shaman, took it upon himself to deal with the crisis. He would make use of his ability to connect with the spirit world. But in these new circumstances, with southern power at work in their lives, he had to communicate with the spirits that were allied to that power. So he took one of the spirits into himself, and became God. Isaac said in his recording that this must now sound foolish, or hard to understand. But he wanted me to know that it was not difficult to believe; people did not know what those spirits, God and Jesus, really were – and they were facing starvation. The way to deal with starvation, the failure of the appearance of animals they depended on, was to make contact with the spirits that controlled those animals, or the weather, or whatever it was that had gone wrong. Someone had to connect with the spirits that were causing the crisis. So Isaac accepted Sala's word, and believed that by being God Sala could solve their problem.

After circling their tent, calling out to them from outside, Sala came in and talked with the family. He explained that he was God, but he was not alone. Ujarak, a relative of his, had now become Jesus. The two of them, Sala and Ujarak, wanted all the people to come and live together in a single large snow house. Only when the people were gathered in one group, in the one place, would God and Jesus be able to bring an end to the hunger, the necessary salvation. Again, said Isaac, it was all very believable. No one was 'wrong', no one 'told lies'; they were just *tammartuvinit*, the ones who had made a mistake.

Isaac's story on the tape did not recount all that happened once people had gathered together in the large snow house, but referred to one particular event. Later, when I asked him to tell me more, he filled in many details. On the tape, though, he wanted to say that those who had made bad mistakes in that snow house should not be judged as criminals. Like everyone else, like he himself, they can see now that they got things wrong. At the time, it seemed to be right. One of the *tammartuvinit* was Ali Apaqquq. Gathered with the others in the large snow house, one of Ali's sisters refused to accept that Sala was God or that any of the things they were saying were true. Urged on by Sala and others, Ali had killed her. Ali was very young, said Isaac, and I had to understand how much people needed to believe, how easy it was to be mistaken.

Sala and Ujarak continued to insist that people stay gathered together in the single snow house. In this way, perhaps by miracles, there would be food and the danger of starvation averted. Many, like Isaac and his family, trusted these men whose role was to find ways of overcoming difficulties by communication with spirits and appeasing them. Those who opposed this were defying some of the deepest and most vital of Inuit beliefs; to oppose was to refuse the established way of dealing with danger and therefore was to add to the risk of starvation. The men and women who followed Sala and Ujarak's urgings to silence those who spoke out against them, or refused to accept the remedy they were proposing, acted in the belief that they were helping to save lives.

Isaac told me that it was not possible to complete the roof of the large communal snow house – igloos, with their reliance on a rising circle of blocks of snow, have a maximum diameter. If they are too wide, the blocks of what should be the central roof are no longer supported, and will collapse. So the people gathered in the way that Sala and Ujarak had urged were exposed to the weather. Also, there was a dire shortage of seal oil, so there were few if any lamps to help keep people warm. This was not sustainable and after only a short time – Isaac did not tell me how long, but I understood it to be days rather than weeks – families left for their usual late winter hunting areas. During that time, though, several Inuit were killed. Ali's sister seems to have been the first; her death was followed by the shooting of the man who had brought a copy of the Bible to the islands. He had opposed Sala and Ujarak, saying he was the real Christian, and refused to join the group in the communal snow house. Another man who refused to go along with the God and Jesus vision was killed soon after the people left the snow house.

———————

After the families were back on the land, spread out in family hunting groups, Sala's family was involved in another incident. Isaac was unclear in his description of this, and reluctant to offer any details – he had not witnessed it at first hand but had heard the accounts of others. Inuit elders were always uncomfortable about describing events they had not seen and experienced for themselves. Stories that were handed down, as parts of history and mythic time, were part of the oral tradition. But things that had taken place in living memory, as the lives of others but not witnessed by the storyteller, were referred to but not told in any detail. To describe experiences that were not one's own was said to be disrespectful and inappropriate – much as the hearsay rule of southern courts restricts what can be given as evidence – but I came to understand the outline of what had happened.

I began to understand that this outburst of religious confusion and violence was an early example of the invasion and disruption of Inuit life by southern institutions. A trader, as part of the trading project, brings families into dependence by offering them goods from the south that they come to rely on in return for the skins that the south wants to buy. But then the trader denies credit to people who are starving. Taking place in the 1940s, this was an early entanglement with the forces of change, with what is now seen as colonial invasion.

I often wondered why Isaac was so concerned that I hear this story, and his part in it. I am sure he wanted to explain to me that he was neither a criminal nor naive. He wanted me to understand that this trust in the men who claimed to be God and Jesus was reasonable and coherent when seen in terms of Inuit beliefs and vulnerabilities at that particular moment. He knew that Inuit were often seen by the Qallunaat as simple, ignorant and, though he would not have used the word, primitive. But it only took a few months living with them for me to realise that their system was rich with sophistication before it was challenged and undermined by changes brought to them from the south. There was nothing naive about the shamanic system, and nothing primitive about the hunting way of life or the economic adaptations being made in response to pressures and demands from the south, any more than Christian beliefs are simple-minded or the economics of trading an achievement of civilisation.

The two systems collided; the new had strong appeal, and the indigenous world looked to its achievements to strengthen its own way of life. The traders wanted fox furs; the Inuit wanted the things from the south that they had come to depend on – tea, tobacco, sugar and, above all, guns and ammunition. The missionaries wanted converts and sought to discredit shamans; the shamans looked to the trinity of new-found spirits to help deal with new challenges and dangers. Isaac helped me to understand that he and his family were at grave risk; there was nothing simple or primitive about the way they turned, as per their intellectual tradition, to the men whom that tradition defined as the ones who could help. There were great dangers, though, as Isaac also wanted to point out: if you make the kind of mistake they made, the consequences can be terrible. The colonial enchanter conjures up a pervasive fear, and can create confusion that opens a path into derangement.

Sala and his extended family were living at a seal hunting camp they often went to in early spring. When the men were away hunting, out on the ice, some miles from the camp, one of the older women, Mina, a sister of Sala's, had a vision of salvation. She declared that as the sun rose Jesus would come and bring salvation to them. She urged everyone to go out onto the sea-ice to meet Jesus, who would travel towards them from the direction of the rising sun. Mina also called out to them to take off their clothes, saying that Jesus would not want them to be covered by anything. Several women and children did as she urged and ran naked towards the sun. Five of them fell and froze to death.

The deaths on the ice seem to have brought the anguished episode of *tammartuvinit* to a close. Sala, no longer claiming to be God, or no longer needing to be in shamanic contact with the new spirits, travelled on the spring ice to the trading post at Richmond Gulf on the mainland to get supplies. Through the trading that year – the ice bridge was strong and lasted all of the spring – word began to spread that there had been some killings on the islands. Isaac told me that a missionary on the mainland travelled out to the islands and went round meeting with families, gathering the story of the events and explaining how the Christian message had been misunderstood. According to Isaac, this missionary was satisfied that there was no further danger and that the best thing would be to leave well alone. But the police had also been told, and they took the view that if the stories were true, and that there had been deaths and perhaps even murder, then they should gather the evidence and, if appropriate, lay charges.

No one involved in this disastrous story sought to hide the facts. Everyone the police interviewed, including Sala and Ujarak, described what they had believed and done. As a result, after several months of fact-finding, those who had been at the centre of the events were charged. This included Sala and Ujarak, who were deemed to have incited murder, and those who were said to have committed the crimes, including Ali Apaqquq and Mina, along with another woman who had urged women and children to go naked out onto the ice. Isaac was not present at the trial, which took place in Richmond Gulf. He was not sure how many were charged. (Court records show that the total was seven.) He knew the outcome, though: Sala, Ujarak and one other man were given gaol sentences of two years, which they served at another community in the Arctic, though Ujarak died in a gaol somewhere to the south before he reached that community. Sala was banned from ever going back to the Belcher Islands. Mina was acquitted on the grounds that she was insane. Ali was also acquitted on the grounds that he was too young to understand what he was doing and deserved compassion. To some extent the court appeared to agree with Isaac – this was a case of being mistaken, not criminal. Isaac told me what he had heard about those who were found guilty. Sala and the others returned to the coast after serving part of their sentences.

Isaac then told me that Sala was still living in Great Whale River, and that the next time I passed through (it was always the jumping-off point for getting to Sanikiluaq) I should visit him. A few months later I was held up in Great Whale for some days. With the help of an Inuit friend I found Sala's house and we made a visit.

In every Inuit village visiting was a central and recurrent part of everyday life. Many conversations with people I met when walking in a settlement would include them urging me with a welcoming imperative: *pulaariarit*, visit. If I said I was going to visit, and used an infix to indicate the future that was within the same day, and then failed to visit that day, I was often gently rebuked. Everyone visited; everyone appeared to be happy to be visited. The ease of this was underlined by the way Inuit went into one another's houses without knocking. At the most, you would say as you came in, *pulaarpunga*, I am visiting. The expectation was that a visitor, like any member of the household, would just walk in and take a seat at the table or on the government-issue couch. As soon as a visitor came through the door children would make sure there was space for them. When I was first in the Arctic I was startled by this way of walking into a house without any ritualistic knocking at doors, asking if it would be alright to come in at that moment. In time I came to appreciate this apparent lack of concern for privacy came from a profound sense that everyone shared the space, be it a home or a part of the land. Even in Great Whale River, a large community, something of a regional centre where I knew only one or two households, and where there were many southerners as well as many Cree families, we walked to Sala's house, opened the door and went in. '*Pulaarpuguk*,' said my friend, we two are visiting.

Sala was sitting at the kitchen table; I no longer remember who else was with him, but there was an older woman, perhaps his wife, who seemed to be shy and even wary of us. She retreated into the background and, to my friend's surprise, did not offer us tea. Sala was quiet and unforthcoming. We explained that I had been living out on the islands and had met many of his relatives. He showed very little interest. Of course, there was an elephant on the table – the whole, vast story of the time he had been God, the killings, trial, imprisonment. He would know that I had heard this story. I think he was waiting for me to ask him about it, but I was overcome by shyness and some discomfort. Perhaps I should not know . . . He left it to me to explain myself, to manage the visit. After a short time I got up saying I had to be going. Sala did not express surprise that our stay had been so short. But as we were heading to the door, he said, 'I will be going back to Sanikiluaq someday soon.' As if to say that perhaps we would meet again, out there on the islands. I did not say, but aren't you banned from going there? Many years later, I heard that he did indeed return, and that no one objected. No doubt the banishment was of very questionable legality. And Sala was in the end able to disregard it. He died there twenty years later.

In 1981 I went again to Sanikiluaq, to work on a film about life on the Belcher Islands. Before the film crew arrived I visited many households to talk about this project, and to see who would be happy to be interviewed, and hear ideas people might have about which aspects of life we should film. One of those I visited was Ali Apaqquq. I thought he could talk about being the son of the famous Flaherty, and that this could help tell the story of the way the Belchers came to be known to the outside world. So I found myself once again visiting the Apaqquq home, sharing thoughts about history, the islands and Saumialuk. I told Ali about the film, and asked him if he would like to do an interview, and talk about his father and perhaps tell the story of Flaherty living on the Belchers as he had heard it when he was growing up. At first Ali seemed uneasy. He said he did not really know the story, and could not remember what people had told him about those first Qallunaat to come to the islands. I worried that he might be wary of an interview because it could take him back to the time of starvation and *tammartuvinit*, and the killing of his sister. I said with great care that the one thing I would like Ali to talk about on film was Saumialuk.

Then, to my amazement, Ali said that he would be happy to describe his father and the house where he had lived. He could talk about the things he had seen for himself. Another example of a wish to avoid saying more than you had seen and heard for yourself. Without thinking, I said that would be wonderful. Then thought: how could Ali have seen or heard anything of Flaherty and his house? I knew that Flaherty had stayed for only a few months. Even if his father had begun his relationship with Ali's mother very soon after running aground on that rocky shoreline, he would have left before Ali was born. But Ali had begun his description, his memories of what Saumialuk and the inside of the house had looked like.

Inuit are good at both telling stories and listening to them. The person speaking tends to be fluent, and can rely on not being interrupted; people do not jump in with some story of their own. They wait until the speaker has come to the end of what they want to say. It is possible, and acceptable, though, to use a pause to ask a question to seek some further clarity, wanting some more of the story that is being told. This is seen as appreciation, not interruption. I waited for a pause and then, taking my courage in my hands, knowing that I risked causing offence, asked a question that was not about the detail of his memories and could have been taken as a challenge to all that Ali was saying. How could he remember seeing these things if he had not yet been born?

Ali was untroubled by my interruption. He could see from inside his mother's womb, he said, and could still remember it well. He told me this as a matter of fact, without appearing to make any special claim for himself. As if all of us could see out of the wombs we were born into long before we came out of them as babies. Later I was to learn that many Inuit had this form of womb memory, and some could even draw a diagram of the womb-home where they lived before birth – a sleeping platform and an entrance way, on the model of a snow house. In one of these memories, recorded by the anthropologist Bernard Saladin D'Anglure in Igloolik, an Inuit elder, Rosie Iqallijuq, recalled a moment in the womb when a dog pushed its nose through the entrance way to her home and vomited towards her as she lay on the sleeping platform. The dog, of course, was the penis of her father, and its vomit her father's semen. Ali did not offer any such memory of intrusion when he was looking out at Flaherty and the first cabin southerners had ever built on the islands, but he had many memories from that time before his birth.

The film crew arrived at Sanikiluaq in the late spring. We went to stay at a seal and bird hunting camp, making trips to small rocky islands where eiders nested in large numbers. The birds created a heap of down, where they laid their eggs. Many of these nests were on raised beaches composed of a mix of fine gravel and ground-up mussel shells. In bright sunlight these beaches gleamed white and blue. Other nests were made among the tussocks of grasses and reeds a few yards inland. Inuit collected eggs and down, as well as shooting some of the ducks. Later, towards the end of the filming, the hunters took us in canoes down to an area to the south. We camped on small islands, hunting seals. Then, one very clear day in early July, when all the ice had gone, Noah Aragutainaq, who was leading this trip, suggested we film Saumialuk's old house, or at least the place where it had been before it burned down.

The site Flaherty had chosen for his cabin was a headland above a steep rocky shoreline. The canoes were pulled up onto the beach – the wooden hulls were given some protection from impact on large and sharp rocks by one of the men taking a position right in the bow, and dropping a plank of wood into the water just as the boat was about to strike the shore, so it rode up onto the plank rather than on the jagged rocks. Noah and the members of his family who were with us led the way to the headland above. We came to an area of level ground, dry and covered with the mix of tussocks and low-lying plants that give a surprising softness and beauty to tundra. Noah walked a short way and then pointed to where the house had been. He stooped and scraped away some loose rocks and earth, revealing the remains of a plank. The others knelt and began to dig into the surface, pulling away a thin layer of vegetation, then digging some more. Soon they were finding things that Flaherty must have brought there. Some pieces of wood, remains of the boards for the walls or roof, were charred, showing that there had indeed been a fire. The most intriguing results of this dig were metal fittings – pieces of pipe, short bolts and thick rusted screws. Everyone was excited by this small excavation of history, exclaiming as they came across each small thing and sharing thoughts about what they might once have been used for. We spent some time there, digging and talking about the place. Noah gathered a handful of the metal items into a bag.

The Inuit made a small fire from the dried twigs of dwarf willows, piling these between two rocks set just a few inches apart lined up with the direction of the wind. This created an intense, confined blaze of heat that brought a kettle to the boil in just a few minutes. We sat on the ground drinking mugs of tea, thinking of Flaherty's life at that cabin, where he and his crew must have spent many hours, looking out to sea, welcoming visits from the Inuit, learning what they could. I imagined Flaherty's time on the Belcher Islands, at this headland, to have been calm, mutually respectful; a first encounter that would turn out to be very unlike much that was to follow. Ali Apaqquq was conceived here, and then had a life drastically shaped by the power of the transforming forces that would follow.

As we left the shoreline below the remains of the Flaherty house, Noah indicated that we would take a circuitous route back to the small island where we had set up our camp the previous day. He said that there would be Inuit staying on some islands a little way to the east of where we were. We should see who might be there.

Sure enough, not long after we pulled away into the complex of sea routes among the islands, we saw a single tent on the land above a long shelving shoreline. Again planks were dropped over the bow as we came to the shore, the canoes were pulled up onto the shingle, and we all jumped out and walked towards the tent. Noah had quickly recognised that this was Ali Apaqquq and his family, so he took with him the bag of things that had been dug out of the ground beside Saumialuk's old house site. I remember that as we came to the open front of Ali's tent Noah called out, '*Ali, ubva ataataviit pirqutiviningit*' – Ali, here are some of your father's former things.

Ali was sitting on the floor of the tent. Noah laid the handful of bits and pieces of rusted and broken metal alongside him. Ali picked up each bit, turning it over, looking at it. Yes, yes, he said, these are from inside the house, I remember this kind of pipe, I saw this, and this . . . He spoke in a cheerful but quite ordinary tone; he did not exclaim in any great surprise or special delight. Everyone listened to what he had to say with interest, hearing what he said as memory, matters of remembered fact.

That night, back at our camp on the small island, the sky became very dark, overcast with an impending storm. I was sleeping in the Aragutainaq tent; the film crew, Ivan and Judy, were in a tent about thirty feet to the side of us, a bit further from the shore. It was very dark but calm as I fell asleep. Then I woke to a crashing noise and the sound of voices shouting. A fierce wind was howling; the flaps of our tent were cracking like whips. The voices came from the camera crew. Along with others from our tent, I went outside. The wind was ferocious, with stinging rain being swept into our faces. Ivan and Judy were using a powerful torch they had brought with them. We could see that they were clinging onto the fabric of their tent, which was in danger of being swept away, and were doing all they could to protect their camera and sound recording equipment. The roar of the wind and the thrashing and cracking of tent fabric filled the air. The Aragutainaq men rushed over to help them and managed to rescue the tent, keep everything dry and make it safe for the rest of the night.

As we got back into our sleeping bags, listening to wind and rain and wondering if our tent was going to withstand this storm, someone began to ask, as if at the beginning of a story, if it might have been a mistake to disturb the ground where Saumialuk had lived. Perhaps Sila, the spirit of the weather, was angry. Who knew what these things from the past might mean. But the storm subsided, Sila was appeased and went away. She is a spirit who, through the meanings of her name, is a force within both climate and the mind – an Inuktitut word for foolish translates as an absence of Sila. We made our way back to Sanikiluaq and the last days of filming. The visit to Ali's tent with some rusted remains of his father's house was the last time I would see him – this was the last time I would be on the islands. He was still living with his family in his tent to the south of Sanikiluaq when I returned to the land of the Qallunaat.

———————

Shamanic religions affirm the possibility of exchange between the human and the spirit domains. They set out the human story as having emerged through transformations, in a time when humans and animals, or humans and any part of the natural world, could be turned one into the other. In this system of beliefs, following this way of understanding life and the land, all humans are part of everything, and everything is part of them. The original stories, and myths of origin, flow into the present, and into the events that shape our lives.

Christian missionaries determined to subvert and displace those beliefs and the practices that they informed, the shamanic way of being in the world. To a very considerable extent they succeeded. Belief in the double power of God and Jesus soon came to be accepted by almost everyone in the Arctic. Faith in and reliance on the shaman were discredited; relationships with the spirit world were all too often turned into a source of shame. Yet for the Inuit of Sanikiluaq, as for Inuit across the Canadian north, and for hunting peoples around the world, to be on their land, hunting, camping, sharing stories and memories was to be in their universe of both place and mind. They might be seal hunting from a modern canoe with a rifle rather than with a kayak and harpoon, but they were still within the space and narratives that made sense of what was there and what people needed to do.

Saumialuk arrived, built his house, conceived a child, and left; he would tell his own stories of this adventure. The people of Sanikiluaq have him as memories of their own. Just as they have the stories of all that happened to them in the following hundred years. God and Jesus came, went away, came back again. Reliance on, even belief in, the porous borders between the different parts of their lives faltered and diminished. Yet the spiritual forces just the other side of that unstable border did not go very far away.

BUT WHAT HAVE WE DONE?

To look out onto the Arctic is to see land that has not been caught in the nets of agriculture and industry, stretching far into the distance without any roads, with just the small pools of buildings that are the new settlements where a few hundred people live in government housing – their hunting territories spreading all around them. The only way for an outsider to travel into these places, or between them, is by air. I would look down from the small planes that were able to land on tiny community runways, low enough to make out pods of beluga whales in long, wide cracks in the ice, but high enough to take in the vast spread of the north, and to feel a mix of awe and delight at its being – or seeming to be – beyond any development or colonial frontier. Southerners like to insist that this is their wilderness. I soon understood that for the Inuit and other northern hunting peoples it is their homeland, a complex of places that have names and stories, the opposite of wilderness.

I had hoped to make a journey that was far beyond my world, and deep into theirs. The less I saw of southern material goods, the more I could be with people dressed in caribou fur and sealskin clothing, the more complete the dependence of those I lived with on the land and all that came from the land, the happier I would be. On one journey I was delighted to notice two of the hunters I travelled with relied almost completely on their own resources: the runners of their sledges had been shaped from long whalebones, the dogs' harnesses and all the traces they used were cut from bearded-seal skin, all their clothing and their sleeping bags were made from caribou skins. On many trips I lived all the time in the language of the Arctic.

This fascination with all that was known, made and understood from within Inuit heritage carried a risk. I would be so inclined towards all that was from the past, from what is known as 'traditional', that I would want to avert my eyes, turn off my thoughts, when confronted with the new. Unlike the Inuit, who welcomed much that came from the south because they could make very good use of it, I wanted to side-step the southern, the modern, my own culture. Which was impossible: I lived, like just about everyone else in the north, in a government-built collection of buildings, benefited from the heat of oil-stoves, and electric lights. Much of what I ate came from the Hudson's Bay Company store, and when I went out hunting, a large proportion of the game that was killed fell prey to a bullet from a rifle that had been bought in from the south. Everyday life meant a constant reliance on material culture that was imported, that represented the presence of the south.

To some extent I could indeed ignore all the things that came from outside, and be absorbed into the aspects of mind that originated for sure in the north: language, memories, stories. But in the end it was not possible to disregard the implications of all those things, and, the more I listened, and the more people talked with me, the more I came to understand that even here, many hundreds of miles from a road, factory or any aspect of urban development, the people were suffering from the dominant forces of outsider power, and both the threat and first realities of dispossession. And, with a paradoxical force, the more people talked to me, sharing what they had experienced and how they felt, the more I began to

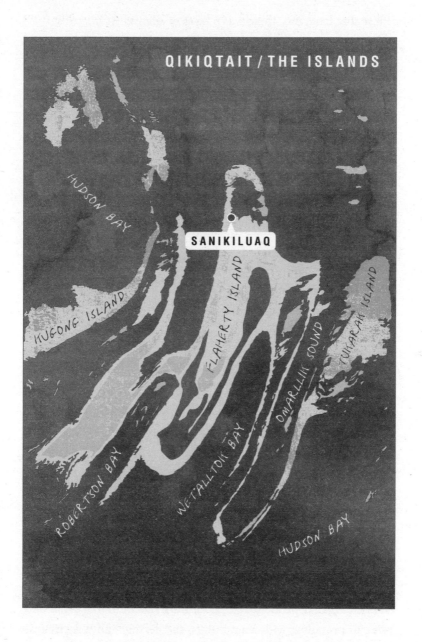

QIKIQTAIT / THE ISLANDS

HUDSON BAY

SANIKILUAQ

FLAHERTY ISLAND

KUGONG ISLAND

TUKARAK ISLAND

OMARLLIIK SOUND

WETALLTOK BAY

ROBERTSON BAY

HUDSON BAY

149

realise that here, too, there was a layer of silence. At first this was a political discovery, a recognition of how imbalances of power and disregard for people's rights were at work even here. It would much later begin to resonate with experiences buried deep within me.

People from the south, the Qallunaat, had overwhelming influence and authority. Everywhere in the eastern Arctic, the Settlement Manager, the government's official representative, was known as *inuliriji*, the one who fixes up the Inuit. And just as I had discovered in Pond Inlet, where I had been living before coming to the Belcher Islands, Inuit in Sanikiluaq had long felt that they must do whatever the Qallunaat asked them to do. When talking to me about their feelings about white people, again and again, like the Inuit in Pond Inlet, they also used the Inuktitut word *ilira*, to express awe (as in relation to ghosts) and intimidation (as in relation to powerful elders or shamans).

In a series of informal one-on-one interviews I did during the first weeks of my time in Sanikiluaq I learned that many events on the islands had been shaped by this *ilira* response to representatives of government, the church, traders and, most recently, schoolteachers. This fearful acquiescence was accompanied by, or had built up in people, a great deal of resentment. Yet the strength of the *ilira*, underpinned and reinforced of course by the actual power of the Qallunaat that the Inuit had dealings with, meant that at least the appearance of compliance continued. Court cases, like the arrest and trial of those who took central roles in the religious upheavals in the 1940s; ever deepening dependence on goods from the south that could only come from trading with southerners; the heating and maintenance of the houses the government had built for the Inuit – all these were manifestations of Inuit subordination to and dependence on southern agencies and agents.

The Qallunaat who based themselves in the north were there either to transform the Inuit and supposedly help them through the confusions of transformation, or to take over possession and management of the land on behalf of the government in the south. The Inuit were to adopt a new religion, learn about the world of the south in schools run by southerners and live more like other Canadians. Christine and I had no such purpose for being there on the islands, and we lived as much as we could outside the norms and attitudes of the Qallunaat. This did not make for easy relations with the other southerners living in Sanikiluaq. The qualities of our house, and the way we lived there, meant that they would not visit us. We were given to understand that our home was not clean enough and it was implied, especially by Don McCoy, the Settlement Manager who had first invited me to the islands, that it was not appropriate for us southern outsiders to be living in intimate proximity with the Inuit.

The one outsider who did like to visit was Ed Horne. Of the three Sanikiluaq schoolteachers, Ed had responsibility for the younger children. He ignored the Qallunaat's disdain for our small shack at the side of the community. Our house was the place where Ed met adult Inuit, and by spending time there he had to some considerable extent dissociated himself from the Settlement Manager and the other teachers (a married couple) with whom he had had a serious falling-out. By thus defying the Qallunaat's disapproval of us, Ed was suggesting that he was not really a Qallunaaq at all – an implication reinforced by his saying to me, as I recall, that he was part indigenous. I remember him telling me an anecdote from his childhood when he and other local children tricked a visiting anthropologist into eating moose droppings. I did wonder, even then, if this was either apocryphal and a chance to poke fun at people like me, southerners who came to the Arctic without a real job, or a story someone had told to him. Yet however much he might have wished not to be identified as one of the Qallunaat, he was very much seen to be one by the Inuit, and treated as such. And the Inuit were right: it would turn out, many years later, that Ed had been born into a white Canadian family in provincial British Columbia. Being a schoolteacher – and due to other factors that I will come to – he had various levels of institutional authority. It was evident that he inspired a good deal of *ilira*.

So Ed Horne was a frequent visitor. I have to be careful about reconstructing or selecting memories in the light of all that transpired. But, as I recall, he would visit just about every day when we were in the settlement. Christine and I made hunting trips that would take us away from Sanikiluaq for several days at a time, and I made quite a few one-day trips that left Christine at the house welcoming visitors, and my guess is that they included Ed. I know that for stretches of time, as during school holidays, he would be away. I also remember with a good deal of clarity how ambivalent I felt about his visits – perhaps to speak of ambivalence is to understate the difficulties: I was often embarrassed by the way he behaved in relation to Inuit who were visiting, and dismayed by the mix of apparent friendliness and ill-concealed competitiveness and, at times, obvious hostility that he showed towards me. He liked to play chess and would regularly suggest that we play. We also shared thoughts about the Inuktitut language.

Ed had a strange relationship to Inuktitut. He had learned the basic grammar, having taken the Mick Mallon course, and was determined to learn as much as he could. I don't remember him ever speaking even a few words of Inuktitut, least of all to the Inuit who came to our house. It may be that this reticence was a result of his not wanting to be heard making the attempt and having the normal, inevitable difficulties in front of another outsider. But I never heard Inuit comment on his Inuktitut skills. People in Sanikiluaq, like Inuit everywhere, were delighted with anyone who had a go at speaking, and would report on this to one another; I am sure that they would have made some comment to me about Ed's Inuktitut if he had been speaking it with them. On a few occasions that I can bring to mind, Ed would talk to me about some aspect of the language, and I remember that once (though only once) he asked me what something meant. Learning Inuktitut did not seem to result in speaking it in his everyday life.

This lack of relationship to the Inuit, as also to the community of Qallunaat, was perhaps the most striking feature of Ed as we encountered and experienced him. It was also evident in the detail of his personality. I remember being very disconcerted by his apparent reluctance to look one in the eye. This was accompanied by a good deal of psychological and physical tension. He was tall and slim, but seemed to lack physical energy. I am not sure of the right words here. I suppose his physical presence was very much a corollary of his intensely cerebral way of being in the world, always suggesting his mental strengths and evidencing minimal interest in anything that was not about ideas or seemingly 'clever'. Christine and I both did our best to be welcoming and easy-going with him. I think he appreciated this, and hence kept on visiting.

In all the time we knew him neither of us ever went into his house. This was a truly remarkable fact. There was no other house in Sanikiluaq that I did not visit (indeed, a game that one of our Inuit friends there liked to play was to see if we could make a visit to every single house in the community, one after the other). And in all the time I was in the north I never came across this apparent, though unspoken, interdict on visiting. Everybody liked to have visitors, and would encourage more visits than were possible. But not Ed. He never suggested I go to his house, and somehow conveyed to me that I should not consider doing so; I never went through the door. I can bring the house to mind, though, and often walked past it. As I remember it, the windows were always covered by some kind of thick curtain – I thought that it must have been blankets that he hung up across every bit of the glass. All light shut out; any possibility of his being seen at home removed.

The dangers of retrospect grow around that house with its thick concealing curtain. We did not look hard enough at what it meant, and now have to suffer imagining what he was doing in that dark concealment he created. But we did think it very odd, peculiar, another way in which Ed was puzzling, weird, and we connected this with feeling uneasy about him, preferring him not to keep visiting, even for the chess games.

Then came the trashing of his house and the apparent suicide of the young man who did it. It happened after I had left the Belchers. As it was told to me, Ed had come back to his house to find that his living room had been smashed up – the lights, the furniture, all his belongings. One of the two young men who had done this then got onto a skidoo and drove out onto the ice, and was never seen again, presumed to have killed himself. Other versions of these events have since been reported, but the two constants are the trashing of Ed's house and the suicide. It is important to bear in mind that this was some years before the outbreak of suicide in the north; it is one of only three cases that I knew about during the ten years – 1971 to 1981 – that I worked there. So it was both shocking and bewildering – and the Inuit who reported the events to me at the time expressed both those responses: they seemed unable to explain how this could have come about, or why that young man should have been so disturbed and self-destructive.

This brings me to the troubling crux of it all, the aspect of the Ed Horne story and events that has haunted me since I first heard of Ed's arrest. Why did we not raise the possibility that he was more than odd and difficult, something other and more significant than a complicated misfit? How did it never occur to us that he might be secretive and hidden because he had something he needed to hide? Once the trashing of his house had occurred, how come no one – as far as I know – sought to get an explanation of the attack on the building and then the suicide? No one seems to have looked at what the relationship might have been between Ed and that desperate former pupil of his. The many revelations about sexual abuse of Inuit and First Nations children that would come to dominate much thinking about the north (and the rest of Canada) in the 1990s, through to today, had not yet come to light. The cases against Newfoundland priests, whose crimes against children were the first to come to the Canadian courts, took place in the 1980s. In the early 1970s people did not think of priests, and still less schoolteachers, as possible sexual predators. It seems naive, in retrospect, or at the least a sign of the times, to have failed to recognise that possibility. It is perplexing: in many ways, for all sorts of reasons. Many of us were intensely sceptical about missionary activity, but our scepticism did not include paedophilia. And the extent of sexual abuse of children in Residential Schools had not yet been revealed. We lacked the knowledge, perhaps we even lacked the language, with which to raise the appropriate suspicions about Ed.

Nor did the Inuit raise them, at least not to me, and perhaps not to one another. I did many interviews with Inuit about the history of the north in which there was extensive focus on Inuit–Qallunaat relationships. In the course of these, people shared with me causes for their dismay and indignation about the way southerners had treated them. They spoke in detail about conflict, at times violent, with Hudson's Bay Company clerks, and in general about the way government had not paid due attention to their needs and feelings. But they did not say anything about what might have been going on behind the blankets across the windows of Ed Horne's house. Was this because they did not know? If so, was that because the children did not tell their parents what was happening? And does this take us back to the significance of *ilira*, the way in which this particular Qallunaaq intimidated the children, and perhaps the parents too?

In crucial ways Ed was very much a Qallunaaq of that era – occupying a position of high status and authority, part of the systematic transformation of Inuit life and consciousness through the school system, and behaving with a good deal of self-importance. That he learned Inuktitut but did not, at the time, speak it in his everyday life, added to this haughtiness, as did the other aspects of his character I have referred to. He held a powerful position, and he took advantage of it. He also benefited a huge amount, I suspect, from the way Inuit at that time acquiesced to southerners, or to those southerners whose role gave them authority within the settlements.

After Ed was charged and taken to a cell in the Iqaluit gaol, Mick Mallon decided to visit him there. Mick told me about this in 2002, some fifteen years after it took place, and I can only suppose that it was an episode he was unlikely to forget. Mick said that he was astonished and appalled to learn of the charges against Ed, but also thought he should look for some degree of compassion. As Mick put it, in his witty way, he, Mick, was 'a heterosexual adultophile', so perhaps he should not rush too fast to judgement on a homosexual paedophile. So he went to the gaol, resolved to be as sympathetic as he could manage. But throughout his visit, he recalled, the only thing Ed wanted to talk about was how outrageous it was that a man like him, with all his education and knowledge, should be subjected to ignorant and uneducated prison guards. Mick was shocked by what he saw as Ed's unrepentant arrogance, looking down, as Mick put it, on everyone from self-styled personal heights. Maybe Mick embroidered the story, but it certainly rang true.

There is much more to be said about these events and all the questions to which they give rise. I don't have answers, though I have thoughts about each part of it – thoughts that lead to some of the most agonising aspects of Inuit recent history.

————————

Inuit elders, and others with extensive experience of the north, point to sexual abuse as a key factor in the rise of youth suicide in their communities. In January 2003, some years after Ed Horne's conviction, Inuit in Cape Dorset, now renamed Kinngait, symbolically burned down the building where Ed Horne had been the teacher. They were getting rid of a physical reminder of the damage he did to their children; I suspect that they were also saying that the damage led to suicides. Ed Horne is often pointed to by Inuit as the direct cause of many deaths in each of the places where he was a teacher. And he is identified as a prime example of those who are responsible for the terrible and continuing epidemic, in which abuse has laid the foundation for suicide among the young.

Ed Horne was a teacher in the Canadian Arctic for almost fifteen years, from 1971 until 1985. He taught in six different Inuit communities, the first of which was Sanikiluaq. He was first arrested in 1985 and in 1986 was charged with sexual crimes against children. He pleaded guilty to molesting eight boys in two settlements, Lake Harbour and Cape Dorset, and was sentenced to a prison term of six years. Subsequently, fifty men in Sanikiluaq and Dorset brought more charges against him. In 2000, he pleaded guilty to twenty-three cases in relation to boys aged between seven and sixteen, and he was sentenced to a further five years. In 2008, he was found not guilty in relation to four more cases. Many of his victims have pressed for compensation from the Canadian federal government. By 2015, awards had been made to 152 of Ed Horne's victims, at a total cost to the government of 36.5 million Canadian dollars.

In January 2015 a former Catholic priest, Eric Dejaeger, was found guilty of the sexual abuse, between 1976 and 1982, of thirty-two children in the high Arctic community of Igloolik – at the same time as Ed Horne was predatory in other settlements. Journalists covering Dejaeger's case reported that he apologised to the court, with some of his victims in attendance (apparently they cried out in grief and fury as he stood there), and asked for forgiveness. He insisted that he would never offend again. The prosecution asked for a twenty-five-year prison term. By comparison, Ed Horne received startlingly short sentences.

Ex-priest Dejaeger and ex-teacher Horne are two of many – some charged and imprisoned, many long since dead or hiding in legal obscurity. In the course of my ten years working in the Canadian north, staying much of the time with First Nation and Inuit families, in remote communities where there were isolated schools and powerful churches, with southerners enjoying extraordinary prestige as they took on their tasks as modernisers and transformers of indigenous heritage, I no doubt met, without knowing it, other frontier paedophiles. Many people across Canada, and indeed the world, were going to learn about the extent of this sexual predation in the Residential Schools to which thousands of Aboriginal children in Canada were sent. Authority at the colonial frontier is exaggerated by geography and politics: the sheer distance from administrative centres delivers to representatives of education and God, when they appear in remote, vulnerable indigenous communities, an almost magical esteem and charisma. The places they work are isolated, and their lives, the buildings within which they live and do their jobs, are further hidden within the isolation. The preconditions for abuse are in place. The victims and their families are intimidated and driven into silence. Southerners, including anthropologists like myself, failed to spot either the abuse or the abusers.

Looking now at what was so well obscured forty to fifty years ago, much is clear that was opaque; this clarity includes the terrible tragedy of Inuit suicides. The teenager who trashed Ed Horne's home was a warning of a virus of anguish, all that was implied by use of the word *ilira*, all the pain that was fomenting. The most dire consequences were still to come.

29 January 2002; twenty years after I was last in the Arctic. The Ontario landscape, at the fringes of Ottawa, spread out in the grey grip of the coldest part of winter. Great heaps of compacted snow and dirt were piled up near the highway from the airport to the city, dumped there by the road-clearing crews after each storm. A fragment of weather and land that made it hard to remember that this was part of a country of great mountain ranges, vast forests and, of course, the tundra, fjords and islands of the Arctic. A taxi took me through a cold and gloomy dusk to the hotel I had booked ahead of time. I was glad to step into its warmth, to begin the recovery from the flight. There was a large, brown Government of Nunavut envelope waiting for me at reception. I took it up with me to my room, thinking here would be the arrangements for the meetings and travel in the coming days. I unpacked, made as much of a home as I could, then sat down at the tiny desk to one side of a large but sealed window, and opened the envelope.

A government official in the new Inuit administration of Nunavut had invited me to visit Iqaluit, the largest town in the eastern Arctic.

Nunavut was the name that the Inuit had given to their territory, a new jurisdiction won through the campaign for their rights to their own lands. It had been set up just two years earlier, in January 1999. Nearly 700,000 square miles of the north, the homeland of 30,000 Inuit, the realisation of a political dream. Now I had a chance to go to the decolonised Canadian Arctic. The invitation arose from publication of my book, *The Other Side of Eden*, but did not include any of the compressed engagements that tend to define book tours. I was being asked to make a return to the north to share thoughts about its history and to meet with some of those who were working in the new Arctic. It was vague, but I was happy not to know quite what anyone had in mind. Here was a chance to experience one of the most ambitious and exciting transfers of power from colonial government to indigenous people anywhere in the world. A chance to be in Canada. A journey back to a nation and landscape – two nations and two landscapes, perhaps – that had shaped my life. It felt strange to be checking into a hotel; this was a place where I had many old friends. But I was needing to be alone, to take my time to re-enter, and I had accepted the offer of privacy, downtown, within walking distance of the first appointment the next morning – 'a round-table discussion' with some of the men and women now working within the Nunavut government.

I opened the brown envelope and took out five pages of typed information. No note about arrangements, and no indication of who this was from. Just a long list, a table of facts. With a row of headings: place, gender, age, method. It was suicide data: a list, for the years 1999 to 2001. The places were all Inuit communities in Nunavut. All of the twenty-five settlements or towns were there, including the ones where I had lived and others where I had stayed or passed through when travelling in the Arctic twenty years before. Some had been – and still were – small villages of a few hundred people. The largest – Iqaluit and Rankin Inlet – numbered more than two thousand. But they were all on the list, every kind of Inuit community. The list was long: dozens of cases. I recognised many family names: the children and grandchildren of men and women I had known, travelled with, lived with, learned from when I had been in their villages and homes.

There was no summary of the facts, no analysis of the cases. Just a line for each one. But it was easy to see the pattern. About two thirds were men, and one third women; all but one or two were between the ages of fifteen and thirty; almost all had died by hanging.

Those who had been aware of these facts might have been surprised at the shock I felt. I had known, of course, about many of the stresses within indigenous peoples' lives, had written about the colonial process and some of the damage it caused, and in the 1970s I had even written one paragraph about a possible future danger of Inuit suicide. But I had not imagined how many lives had been taken in this way, how long a list they would make. By the time I had read to the end of the last page, I knew that this represented a suicide rate at a terrifying level. I also could see that there was a spread across the north: every community had more than one case – the most isolated as much as those that had long been administrative centres. I was reading through a catalogue of anguish, of disaster.

I sat at that desk for a long time, looking in bewilderment at the names of communities where I had had the happiest and most magical of times; reading again and again the age, the method – saying to myself the names of these young men and women, these boys and girls – who had hanged themselves. Imagining what this must mean for the families, the communities, the north; realising that here was a dreadful reshaping of history. I felt chilled with shock: the cliché of such moments was for real – my blood ran cold.

Using a few basic facts about overall Arctic population and doing some simple maths, I worked out that the Inuit suicide rate revealed in this list was at least fifty per hundred thousand; the rate for young Inuit men was at least a hundred per hundred thousand. Suicide rates have long been expressed in these terms – the total number of deaths in a year against the total population. Calculations for very small communities are statistically strange, since a few cases can give very high overall rates. I knew, though, that the rate for Canada as a whole was about twelve per hundred thousand, and for the UK about fourteen. The numbers might be unreliable as statistics, but they screamed out a terrible reality.

I also felt that these sheets of paper were confronting me with questions I had to face, accusing me of something I had to answer for. Not paying attention to, not writing about, the north as it transformed after I was there? Failing to act on the first warning of this, when word came from Baffin Island in the 1970s that two young women had killed themselves? Not seeing something that spoke to this transformation, that may have been the beginning of these facts? Not interrogating deeply enough all that I had known about Ed Horne? Or something more elusive than these questions? A collusion in silence? Was it a result of an absence of framework that would point to possible abuse? A failing within the anthropology of that time? My tendency to focus on the elders and their life on the land? Or something more personal that led to my myopia?

———

I made two journeys to Iqaluit to understand the reality behind the list of suicides. I met with men and women I had known many years before: the son of Anaviapik who had often taken me out on the ice with him was there, one of Anaviapik's daughters, now living with her own family. Peter Kattuk from Sanikiluaq was now a minister in the new government. I went to his office and we talked for a long time about the journeys we had made together, looking at a map of Qikiqtait, the islands, pinned on the door to his office to see the exact routes and camping places, the sites of so many stories. Peter also told me about the rise of suicide among the Sanikiluaq young. The joy of shared memories, the thinking back to joyous times, was undercut by the pain of those young people's deaths. I met with other Inuit in Iqaluit who were working at all levels of the new government. They too wanted to tell me about their dismay, fear and grief; every single person I talked with shared their experience of the suicides. All had close relatives and friends who had died; many spoke of their own struggle with despair and times when they too had thought they may as well kill themselves.

I was led into the awful details. Hangings took place in the home. The standard, government housing for Inuit families has a closet built into each bedroom. Those intent on suicide were using a rope attached to the rail in these closets. But these are not rooms with high ceilings; the roof of the closet is not much above head-height; there is no drop. Death could be achieved only by drawing up the legs, effecting suffocation. This could not be easy: the suffocation would happen if there was a sustained and strong pulling downwards; to succeed depended on a very high level of determination. One woman, whom I had known as a joyful and chatty child, described her own attempt, the pressing of the rope, the loss of breath, and then, unable to get it done quickly, her decision to go on breathing, to wait for another time. I was to learn that there were many such attempts that failed, or where the time it took allowed for a change of mind. Where it did succeed, it would be the immediate family that would find the body in the closet, and have to suffer the anguish of both the death of a close relative and the image of this slow, resolute way of dying.

I spoke with a cabinet minister in the new government who described to me the grief that is expressed at the funerals of the young who have died in this way, conveying the mix of incredulity and desperation that the death of the young must always cause. He talked about how his own family had felt when one of their children had killed himself. He described the cries of grief that lasted all through the child's funeral. Then, as if thinking aloud, he said that this grief was a mistake, it should be avoided. Why? Because it is a message to the other young people, showing them what a big effect their death can have, how the parents, all the family, will be so hurt, will cry out for them. And this, he went on, maybe encourages suicide; this could be what they want, what they think they need – this cry of pain from parents. And we must come up with some measures, some new ideas about what to do. As he explained, I understood that when he said 'we', he meant the government, the whole wide community of people that was Nunavut. He sat at his desk, looking out of the window, sharing despair at the memory of his child who killed himself and his doubts about ever finding a way through and out of this dark place.

Yet the north still gleamed. During the first trip to Iqaluit I went out onto the sea-ice, taken by a hunter on a sledge hauled at lurching speeds by a snowmobile. I sat on the gear lashed to the sledge, turned my back to the cold wind, and looked out onto the frozen bay. The sun of early spring created the magic of Arctic light. It was the north as it had always been. People going back and forth to look for seals at the floe edge; a supply of seal meat, Arctic char and caribou coming into the community. To be heading out onto the land, or to spend time visiting with old friends in town – here was the familiar beauty of the north. But I could not get away from questions and thoughts about the unhappiness that must lie deep within any community where so many of its young do not want to live. One couple summed this up for me in their own words, from their own point of view: 'Every day we wonder whose death we will be hearing about, who in our family will be next. We wonder when we will next be at one of those funerals.'

I did more research into the problem of youth suicide, looking at data from many parts of the world, speaking with psychologists and anthropologists who had been looking for both the facts and their explanations. The rates I had been shown for the Canadian Arctic were part of a global trend, a crisis in many Aboriginal communities. The same flow of events was being described in Alaska, Greenland, Australia, much of Canada. Young people, especially young men, had suicide rates of anything between seventy-five and two hundred and fifty per hundred thousand, many multiples of those in the same nations who were not from First Nation or Aboriginal families. Again and again it was the descendants of hunter-gatherers who had the worst stories to tell. Since the 1980s, steadily increasing through the following two decades, large numbers of young people were killing themselves. And for all who succeeded, there were many more who made suicidal plans or attempts. In some studies in the United States, as in my own findings for the Canadian north, as many as one in three young people said that they were suicidal. The studies also revealed that the attempted suicide rate was the same for young women as for young men.

———————

The human mind depends on speaking and listening, hearing and telling stories. If there is silence, an absence of words, a failure of speaking and listening, then there is much about who we are that we cannot know. Not everything in all parts of life finds its way into stories that are told, but almost all that does find its way into our minds comes from some form of storytelling. And the telling of stories within the family is both the starting point and essence of what can grow in our minds.

History reveals itself in the family. Absence of history can make the family a painful and even a dangerous place. The young are not able to name this pain or speak to this danger; instead they can begin to feel, and to be overwhelmed by, a set of absences – there is no joy, no meaning, no way out, no hope, no place in this world for themselves. From the outside, they may look happy much of the time, have many things they do and could be doing, and have a very rich and apparently meaningful place in the world. But the feelings sweep up from below all these appearances, the surfaces of everyday.

Thus silence in the home can leave a void in the child. This is an internal echo of the void that is outside them. Unspoken grief, feelings of helplessness, anger – all these make sounds that the child takes in and holds and even begins to need. These can be sounds that do not set out meanings, since they are coming from a determination not to give meaning, yet they are shaping the mind. This determination may come from the best of instincts, a loving wish to protect the child; or from the impossible burden of historical traumas; or may come from sadness and anger that cause a direct rejection of the child. There may be a crucial difference between unspoken personal grief and the silences of historical trauma, but the same kind of damage will be done.

Across the north where I had spent time listening to and learning from hunting peoples, abuse had taken several forms. Colonial power and regulations meant that the land and ways of living on and from the land had been placed under a new and alien system of governance. This was an abuse of indigenous rights and customs. Those who disregarded or broke the new rules were at risk of punishment. Denial of credit at a trading post; arrest by a Qallunaaq police officer; trial and prosecution by a judge and jury from the south. These events showed to the Inuit – were designed to show the Inuit – that they were no longer in charge of life in the north. This was an abuse of power. Teachers and missionaries insisted that they, not the people who lived in the north, knew the truth about all the most important matters. This was an abuse of the mind. Mining companies, oil and gas corporations, logging contractors came to the parts of the north where they could develop the resources they valued, and did all that they needed to do without regard to either the land or the people who had lived there and known it for generations. This was a violation of those people, and of the land itself. Furthermore, some of those who represented, advocated and implemented these abuses gave themselves the right to abuse the bodies of the children they said they were there to teach or to save.

Sexual abuse of children may be different in crucial ways from other forms of abuse: it is a direct assault on the most vulnerable. But it has a critical relevance to all other damage done: child victims of abuse are rendered unsure of themselves, and thus given an acute sensitivity to all the forms of damage that they might then face. Sexually abused children can find themselves driven into and then caught in the deepest of silences, while needing, more than anyone else, to be cared for and heard and given a chance to heal. The wider abuses – of heritage, land and belief – mean that their chances of being given the care, offered a chance to have a voice, are minimal. Damage to the society makes for silence, grief and anger on all sides. Those who would expect to have the job of passing on knowledge, insight, beliefs and all the skills that are the heart of a culture have been undermined. Those who have been abused devalue themselves. Parents have been caused to doubt the worth and validity of all that they were raised to be, and have lost confidence in all that they should be passing on to their children. Or the children have been persuaded that the parents have nothing of real value, no relevant truth to offer. So the line from the older to the younger generation is broken. Each is caught on their side of the line – the old not able to be parents as they would have wished to be, the young not able to look to parents for all that young people need. Thus the meaning of life as it was, as it should be, as each side of the generational divide needs it to be, is lost in uncertainty, grief and silence. The next generation is left with absence of attachment, and a longing for the things that they deeply need but, as small children, find that they cannot have.

———————

In the absence of meaning there is a need to find it, or to find some place where meaning can be found. And nowhere is more likely than in feelings for another person. It is in the embraces of love where the deepest, most intractable solitude can be escaped and where the worst voids can appear, for once, for some moments, to be filled. These moments of love are part of a larger, widening possibility: here at last there is a sharing of thoughts, a meeting of body and mind at least in defiance. Here the very impossibility of sharing can be shared. The mutual sympathy of hearing from one another when so often there has seemed to be no such possibility.

These moments suggest that it could all be otherwise: if this love continues, it promises an end to the void – here is a place where steps into the world, back into the landscapes of meaning, can be taken. Thus the creation of a sense of place, of family, the building of a home, a sharing of minds seems possible. There can be a dream that is spoken out loud. In these ways, the relationship, the pairing in love and for love, delivers meaning. A meaning that feels like the sudden breathing of air, the flow of energy in the blood. A meaning that ensures that there is, perhaps for the first time, or the first few times, a feeling that life is worth living.

Fusion of two young people in this shared discovery of life creates loss of self as well as discovery of meaning. The two go together: they are what is found in young love by those who have found so little elsewhere. Thus it is that the young in societies that have experienced the greatest assault and undergone the most widespread and profound collective loss are the ones who are most desperate to find meaning in romance.

The relationship in these circumstances carries an enormous load. All meaning comes from the relationship. And almost no relationship can bear this – least of all those that take place on colonial frontiers. These are troubled individuals, not settled couples who have co-created a long life together. They are teenagers for whom the basis of a love affair is without any connection to shared economic or even domestic life. Their need *for* one another, and what they need *from* one another, is the meeting of all needs – urgent and abstract, fierce and often desperate. Yet the very reasons that explain the intensity of the relationships also mean that they have very little chance of stability.

Relationships in many indigenous communities are taking place in a wounded and fractured world. In societies where great social losses have been endured, where the land, home and belief systems have been invaded, where just about every corner of life has been corroded or demolished, where those who sustain wellbeing do so in defiance of much by which they are surrounded – in these places, under these conditions, romantic and sexual mores become frantic and chaotic. There is profound instability in each level of relationship, converging, as one would expect, on love itself. A great need for love is matched by its great unreliability. The very place that seems to offer solace is where solace is least likely to be sustained. So the young are the ones who suffer most the set of forces that have been at work on their societies.

The suicide data for Inuit and other indigenous communities that I have seen do not include the surrounding or underlying circumstances; some refer to drug and alcohol links, but not personal narratives, the story of the life at the time of the death. I spoke with many Inuit about their own stories, the circumstances that they say pushed them to an attempt, and with many relatives and friends of those who had succeeded. Again and again I heard about relationship break-up; the breaking of the heart that was transformed into the breaking of the wish to be alive. One Inuit elder, whom I had known since she was a teenager, spoke and wrote to me many times about her life in the north, and the way the suicides had borne down on her life. She had been a mother, community member and social worker in one large community, and she told me that 'it is always love, disappointment about love'. Many teenagers she had known just wanted to believe in their relationships, 'even though there was nothing they could trust'.

The young experience what has happened to their communities in amplified, concentrated form. This is where they meet history, and where history goes to work on their future. In Aboriginal societies, where history comprises so much deep-seated and ongoing attack, the young pay with their hearts. Human beings insist that there be meaning to life, but when a life appears to have no possible meaning, in this awful darkness, ideas of death can feel all too welcome. If many others – close relatives, best friends, neighbours in a small community – are choosing death, then there is a further welcome, a vicarious familiarity with the choice.

There are individuals who do not have the opportunity or the facility for these intense but unstable relationships. Or societies in which repression of relationships, at least of romance and sexuality, is as much a part of everyday life as a promiscuity of relationship may be in the kind of milieu I have been describing. But here, the same kind of force can be at play: the need to be able to load into love all possibilities for wellbeing. This can amount to looking for what is not allowed or not available. Then we can imagine the desperation that comes with an idea of emptiness and hopelessness stretching ahead, with no prospect of relief, of an ending. And thus there can be an image of, even a falling into a longing for, an end to it all that is made possible, conceivable, by an end of self. Where love must carry all the load of life it is likely to break down under the weight of itself.

In the summer of 2018 I made a return journey to the high Arctic. I flew into Pond Inlet on an August afternoon, the sky heavy with low cloud and drizzle. Alex Anaviapik, one of Simon Anaviapik's many grand-daughters, had for some time been encouraging me to visit, and I had been in touch with Philippa Ootoova, a Pond Inlet friend from decades before. But Alex had been born long after I had last been there, and I did not expect Philippa to take on the responsibility of making arrangements for me. It was forty years since I had lived in the high Arctic. I walked from the plane to the single small building that is the Pond Inlet airport expecting to feel like a ghost, thinking it might have been a mistake to come back here, to expect that I could rediscover connections that might belong in a profound and forgotten history. But as I came into the airport building I saw a small crowd of people, and realised that they had come to greet me. I may have doubted the longevity of relationships; they did not.

Right away I saw a face that was deeply familiar – it was Anaviapik, or his double, his exact face and even expression, a bit older than I remembered him. But he would now be over a hundred, and I knew that he had died a long time ago. The man came to me, and caught me in a tight hug, holding to me, looking at me, tears in his eyes. It was Jayko, Anaviapik's youngest son, the one he often said was his favourite child. I had known him well, though he was often away at boarding school when I was going to his father and mother's house every day for my Inuktitut lessons. His absence, the intensity with which his father missed him, may have been one of the reasons for Anaviapik's adoption of me, so much the child who needed to be taught everything. I remembered Jayko as quick-witted, bright, respectful of his heritage but also very modern. The last time I had seen him he was eighteen years old, and he had grown to look just like his father.

Alex was Jayko's daughter. She introduced herself. Others came up and shook my hand, saying how happy they were that I was back. One of these was a woman in her forties. She held my hand in greeting and told me she was Tina Inukuluk. 'I always heard about you from my father,' she said. 'He told us that he helped to take care of you, so I can do that for you now. You must tell us if there is anything you need.' Inukuluk was another of Anaviapik's sons, and he had indeed spent a lot of his time taking me out hunting, teaching me, helping me to understand life. We had made dog-team journeys together, camped out at all times of the year; his house, which was one of the smallest in Pond Inlet, no more than a one-bedroom shack, had been one of the best of all homes to visit. I remembered that Inukuluk and his wife Sippora had had three young children; Tina must have been born about a year after I left. I stood there at the airport, surrounded by people who saw me still as part of their family. My adoptive relations.

Tina offered to take me visiting. Who would I like to see? Over the week that I was there we went to many houses, spent time sitting at kitchen tables, on the single couch, in homes that were modern in the obvious ways – a large TV, computers where people were busy checking emails and sharing news on Facebook, and mobile phones at hand as much as in any other part of the world. There were also the indicators of modern inequality. Some houses were large and equipped with expensive furniture and, most important of all, with new skidoos, canoes and even four-by-four pickups parked outside. Most houses, though, were small, a little dilapidated, and just the same as the houses I had known and where I had stayed in the 1970s. Other things had not changed: the warmth of each house, the gentle welcome, the humour, the wish to share stories, memories and, of course, food. Also, almost everyone I met spoke to me in Inuktitut – even though now, after a full generation of schools with their southern teachers and curricula, almost everyone could speak fluent English.

The second day I was there Tina asked me if I remembered Mukpa. Of course I did: he had been an impressive hunter with a sharp sense of humour, remarkable for his strength and hunting skills, and, in his thirties, one of the last of the younger generation to use a dog-team. He and Anaviapik, with two dog-teams, had taken me with them on a three-week journey from Pond Inlet to Arctic Bay and back. The journey there had been across a range of mountains that separated the two settlements at the north tip of Baffin Island. This had taken a week. After a short stay in Arctic Bay, we had chosen to return round the shoreline better to be able to hunt for seals. Many things went wrong. On the first night out of Arctic Bay, while we all slept in a snow house, the dogs managed to break into a separate, very small snow hut where we had cached all our supplies. They ate everything. We continued on with only the sugar and tea that we had kept with us overnight. At one point, Mukpa scraped out the smears of grease that had accumulated in the Coleman stove we were using, and made a soup. It was a strange mixture of fat and sugar, and very welcome. There was an alarming moment during a break for tea when Anaviapik turned to me, looked into my face, and said, 'You're so thin!' I looked at him, and saw that his eyes appeared to be very large, and his cheeks sunken. He also said, in a matter-of-fact voice, 'We probably won't make it back to Pond Inlet.' Some of the dogs collapsed and were set loose to fend for themselves. But thanks to Mukpa remembering that his family had stored much of a bearded seal under rocks at a former campsite that was along the fjord where we were travelling, we found food, rested and at last made our way back. That happened in May 1972.

I have written about this difficult journey before, and had often thought about it, remembering its details and thinking about its implications. The calm, untroubled stoicism of the two men; the way critical decisions were made; and the remarkable skill with which they dealt with each part of the unfolding crisis – from building a snow house each night in blowing snow, however tired they must have been, to contriving to generate scraps of food. Their ease with and within the land, even when the land seemed to be lit with dangers. And the detail, the depth, of their knowledge. In the few weeks of that trip to and from Arctic Bay, I saw and learned a great deal about what Inuit travel and hunting meant, and what was required. I remember that when at last we had reached safety – a hunters' cabin a few hours from Pond Inlet – and were settling down for the last night before getting home, Anaviapik said to me, 'And now you know what it was like in the old days.' But he and Mukpa had been showing me what it was like in all times.

Tina told me that Mukpa was still living in Pond Inlet, and said that she was sure that he would be very happy to see me. We went over to Mukpa's house – one of the older buildings – and found him sitting at his kitchen table wearing shorts and a loose T-shirt, surrounded by some of his numerous family – his wife, two sons, a daughter-in-law, some grandchildren. He was now in his eighties, and suffered from severe diabetes. One of his legs had been amputated at the knee; the other was swollen and black in colour. Yet his eyes sparkled with enthusiasm, and when Tina had explained who I was, he shouted with excitement. I sat opposite him and right away began to reminisce about our journey back from Arctic Bay. At first in general terms – yes, it was a difficult trip, things sure went wrong, we were very hungry. Then he chuckled over details he brought to mind. Then I said I remembered that three of the dogs had died. No, no, he said, five, and he proceeded to name them all.

Mukpa had held every part of our journey in his mind. The decisions that had to be made about the route, the exact twists and turns of the way through the mountains. Things that were said. What we were wearing. Everything. And all the time remembering with gleeful bursts of laughter, taking pleasure in the memory. The next day I found a tourist map of the region, showing the northern end of Baffin Island with all the area that we had travelled together, and took it to him. It was a crude map, designed to give visitors an impression of the land and not much more. But Mukpa drew onto this map each part of our route, making a line first from Pond Inlet to Arctic Bay over the mountains, indicating which fjords and valleys we had followed as we reached into and then climbed up to the heights of the land, and which pass we had got through to begin the journey down towards the sea-ice that we could follow to Arctic Bay. He marked each of the spots where we had built a snow house. Then the details of the return journey, round the headlands, along the shore and the detour out onto the sea-ice to the north. The place where we had been caught by the storm and where we had built snow houses on the sea-ice. And the old campsite where he had pulled out the pieces of cached bearded seal. He took his time, correcting himself when he saw he had not got it quite right, squiggling over a section of route that he saw he had got wrong and then marking in a new, corrected line, all the time recalling events, things that were said, the state of our hunger, and chuckling at the memories, at the humour of it all.

Mukpa's wonderful memory and sparkling way of remembering reminded me of the people, and the life, that I had been lucky enough to get to know. I sat close to him; Tina stayed nearby ready to help with translations when I got confused or stuck. Younger members of Mukpa's family listened, joined in, and brought us cups of tea. I was taken back to the hundreds of hours I had spent, forty years before, with families in Pond Inlet and Sanikiluaq, visiting, listening and learning. Canada, along with all the other nations, has taken over the Arctic and set about 'developing' the lives of Arctic peoples with their commitment to 'progress'. That pair of one-word oxymorons, 'development' and 'progress': these are the terms that denote and urge changes to ensure that life becomes 'better', richer, more modern. Yet the changes they bring include inequality, breakdown of community, unprecedented forms of poverty and despair, and loss of the core and essential values – respect for one another and the land. And the undermining of belief in 'traditional' memory and the people's own history – all the stories that most needed to be told.

I walked through Pond Inlet, visited many homes, talked to elders I had known when we were very much younger, and to those who were the children and grandchildren of men and women I had loved, travelled, hunted with and learned from many years before. I saw and heard about the consequences of development, the progress that had been made. The question that people kept asking me, young and old alike, was: do you think it was better back then, when you were there, in that time when, as people kept putting it, *inummaringulaurpugut*, we were real Inuit? My answer was that I could not say, I had been away for too long. A relative of Anaviapik's whom I had known well in the 1970s did not like this answer of mine. 'You do know,' she said. 'You must remember how happy everyone was, and how strong. And how we shared with one another.' Then she said, 'They sent me away to school, so I did not live that life. But you saw it. So you know it was better, much better.'

I was back in the place where I had been young, where I had been given a home, where I had discovered the depths and beauty and welcome of the Arctic. Where I had travelled across the land with hunters, and sat in their houses and listened to stories, shared their food, learned a language that had never ceased to define who I was or how I thought. A language that had again and again turned up in my dreams however far I was from the north, and however long it had been since I was there. But now this place was transformed; or I was being asked to look again at what I had seen, and rethink, revisit, in ways that were both difficult and dismaying.

Simon Mirqusak, an important elder in the new Pond Inlet, whom I had known as a young man, reminded me of a trip we made to the mouth of the Iqaluit River, in an area where his parents and grandparents had spent much of their lives. The river flowed out of a series of lakes, no more than a mile inland. Large numbers of Arctic char spent the winters under the ice of these lakes. Then, in late June, as the ice melted and broke and the river filled with its spring flood, the char migrated down the river to return to the sea. We had gone on sledges over the sea-ice from Pond Inlet to Iqaluit, camped on the shore near the river mouth, and walked out onto the ice that still covered the river's estuary. Using narrow cracks in this estuary ice, we had lowered lures into the water below, and pulled out the char as they grabbed and caught on the hooks. The water was teeming with fish. In no more than an hour we had caught as many as we needed. Remember how easy it was to get there, and how many fish there were? Simon asked this, to set up his answer: 'Well, you can't go there any more. The ice isn't there.' In the spring, the Iqaluit River, and its abundance of seaward-migrating char, now pours into an open estuary, free of ice. Much of the journey from Pond Inlet down into the fjord of the Iqaluit territory is so broken and softened by the middle of June that any attempt to take a sledge on that route is dangerous. What used to be reliable knowledge, or the knowledge that made a part of the environment reliable, was no more. This was global warming.

Everything has changed, is changing. I thought that Simon, like everyone else I spoke with, was saying that there were changes of all kinds, with global warming both an example and, at the same time, a metaphor. The one thing that hasn't changed, Simon told me, is the way that the Qallunaat keep to themselves, as if they were more important than the Inuit, and continue to hold onto as much power as they can.

Each late spring, when the ice is just good enough to travel on, pods of narwhal appear at the floe edge, where the fast ice ends and there is a mix of open water and moving, broken ice pans. Hunters travel out to this ice rim of their lands, hunting seals and waiting for a chance to kill a narwhal. I remembered being there in June 1973, standing with a young hunter on the firm ice and watching a narrow pool of open water that had been defined by a maze of moving, broken pans. In the distance, further out to sea among the moving ice, we could hear the calls of narwhal – at times a series of high, staccato squeaks and then a low mooing sound, as if a herd of cattle was trapped out there. We stood, listening, wondering in which direction the narwhal might be moving. Suddenly there was a surge in the water in front of us, no more than twenty yards away, and the backs of some six or seven narwhal came out through the surface, in the rolling, arching movement of whales as they come up to breathe. We could hear the rush of breath that they exhaled through their blow-holes. They stayed close to the surface, circling in the pool of water. The young man next to me was carrying a rifle slung over his shoulder. To my surprise he did not begin to move it, to make ready to shoot. Instead, he reached inside his parka and pulled out a camera. He took a series of photographs. Then the narwhal, perhaps seeing us there and noticing some movement that alarmed them, dived back down and were gone. That young man had become an elder in Pond Inlet. I visited him a few days before leaving. He told me, with quiet pride, that he had twice gone to work for a spell for oil companies, at the drilling sites in the high Arctic islands, but had otherwise lived only by hunting. He had returned the day before from the floe edge – he offered me a plateful of fresh boiled seal meat that he had brought back.

At the beginning of August the sun does not set, even at midnight. Most people would sleep for much of the day then be up, visiting and hunting, through the night – the ice in front of the settlement had been fractured and opened enough for seals to appear in the water close to shore, and for a fisherman to cast a line and set a short gill net in wide patches of open water. Two days before I was due to leave, tides and winds pushed the ice away from the shore, and it became possible to launch a boat and, navigating through and around the flotillas of broken ice, head far out into the sound between Pond Inlet and Bylot Island. Everyone was filled with excitement; many kept an eye on the new leads that would allow the narwhal to come close to the settlement; some prepared their boats and hunting gear to be ready to set off as soon as the narwhal were spotted; others went far out into the sound, anticipating where the narwhal would travel.

I watched the hunters on the shore, went down and talked with the men who were setting the first net I had seen, marvelled at the gleam of the first two Arctic char that they caught, and followed the movements of the small boats in which hunters were threading a route across the sound. I watched them making their cautious way towards a pan of ice where some seals were basking; I could just see two boats that were far out in the ice. This was not the telling of stories about some other, perhaps better time; here were the Inuit out on their land, their ice and sea, fishing, stalking seals, hunting for narwhal. Everything I was watching, everyone out there on the shore or making their way among the moving ice floes, depended on immense bodies of knowledge, a huge set of skills. All eyes were focused on the kill, for it would become the food that everyone liked the most. It was the middle of the night, with the sun low across the horizon to the north-west. Development and progress were all the time contested by memory; meanwhile they had not erased knowledge.

————————

Nuna is the Inuktitut word for land. When they use this word, however, Inuit mean more than is conveyed by the English word 'land'. *Nuna* includes the terrain, rivers, lakes, the seashore and the water or ice they travel through and across as part of using their land. It also includes all the creatures they find in these different places, all that they know to be living there. When the hunters in Pond Inlet, in the middle of that August night in 2018, set a net for char, stalked a seal on a pan or launched a boat into the mix of open sea and breaking ice, they relied on all that is in the mind, and all the time they had occupied their land.

The mind of those who look to their lands for meaning, and who rely on all that they know of their land to be able to find, kill and process the food they have long depended on, is who they are. In the past forty years the Inuit, like so many indigenous peoples, have had to face the most painful challenges. They have had to grasp, cope with and, often, do everything in their power to resist 'development' and 'progress'. Those seeking to challenge the dangers urge them to tell their own stories in their own way. Stories about how they lived, what they know, the experiences they have had as they hunted, gathered, camped, shared all that they knew and all that they harvested.

I stood once again with Inuit on the shores of the Arctic, looking out at their land, all that the land has been and can be. And I heard the new generation of elders, the men and women who had been teenagers or children when I had last been to the north, tell me that this is where they can hope to see the answers to the most agonising of questions about life and death.

BERLIN

In early 1992 my mother phoned to tell me that she had received a disturbing letter from a lawyer based in Israel. It was written in German, and with some legal language that she said she could not understand. It asked if she was the daughter and perhaps the heir of Tina Schäfer, and if so, could she give proof of this? If she was, and Tina Schäfer was no longer alive, could she give evidence of her death? She sounded anxious, and kept telling me that this was a letter she did not want to receive and did not know how to respond to. Why would anyone need to know details about her family history? It must be to do with family property. She kept saying she did not want anything to do with such things. She asked if I would take a look at the letter.

I found that this letter, the mysteries it seemed to imply, its sudden evocation of the past and the dead, filled me with a strange energy: a possible window on people and places that I found myself eager to throw open. It was evident from the legalese in the letter that this was indeed about property, with a reference to a Jewish organisation that was engaged in restitution for Holocaust survivors and their heirs. I urged my mother to find any documents that would help prove who she was, and to take a photograph of her mother's grave, with its clear lettering showing the name, Ernestine Schäfer, with dates of her birth and death — perhaps on the view that things carved in stone are more definitive than pieces of paper. An irony of this is that my grandmother had always declared she wanted to be cremated, but when it came to the decision, my parents decided she must be buried, as Jewish law requires, in the Sheffield Jewish cemetery. Thus – against her wishes – she came to have a clear, undeniable headstone, proof of her life and death. The strength of the evidence, tombstone and papers to prove that Ernestine Schäfer was indeed my mother's mother led to another letter from the Israeli lawyer. My mother forwarded it to me.

It explained that my mother's grandfather, Hilel Badian, the man after whom I had been named, had owned a block of flats in Berlin. Number 36, Gleimstrasse. This had been seized by the Nazis in 1934. He had died in Auschwitz, along with one of his two daughters. The surviving daughter was Tina Schäfer, my Oma, and my mother was her only child. So, in theory, she was heir to this large property. She had never known of its existence, and had not been told by her adoring grandfather that he had invested in Berlin real estate. Presumably he had not told his daughter about it either. Since my mother was his only grandchild, this seemed an odd reticence, though it may be that the events of the unfolding horrors moved with such surprising speed that he did not know what to tell anyone. It turned out he had owned this block of flats for only two or three years. By the time he might have wanted to explain to his heirs what his assets amounted to, they – both the assets and indeed the heirs – were being taken from him. So the first my mother ever heard about her possible inheritance was in these letters from Israel, in 1992, as a consequence of the fall of the Berlin Wall.

I went to Berlin to see this block of flats. It was a huge building, grey and drab with neglect, sitting on a whole city block. I stood across the street and stared, trying to imagine my grandfather making a visit if only at the time he bought it; then the Nazis taking it over, and no doubt carrying out a survey. It looked as though nothing had changed, no coats of paint or repairs to the brickwork. The street was quiet. I wanted to go into the building, up its stairway, into some of the flats. As if I could walk past the dilapidated front door and pass through time. In a strange lurch of the mind I felt an impulse to move in there myself, to occupy the past, the past that perhaps should have been mine. To leapfrog over the Nazis, the murders, the traumas within me.

I walked to the front of the block and looked at its row of buttons, some with names beside them. It comprised over thirty units. Then I went round the back, and was surprised to find a gym that had been set up through an entrance into what I think was a basement. There was also a flower shop, open, with a small stand of blooms and plants outside a rather grimy plate-glass window. A young woman stood just inside its door. I guessed she worked there. I decided to buy some flowers from her, then was overcome with a surprising shyness – or, now that I remember that moment, with a fear of being overwhelmed. Did this building, or a large portion of it, really belong to me?

It was run-down, neglected, but stood within the newly fashionable Prenzlauer Berg. I realised that it must be worth an enormous amount of money. An entire city block, over thirty apartments, the gym and shop . . . The potential for development. I went back to England, went to visit my mother, and told her what I had seen and how valuable this was.

She seemed to be glad that I had made the journey and could describe it to her, but she did not want to think about the value, the money it might represent, the extraordinary change it could cause to her life. She said she had no interest in getting ownership,

36 GLEIMSTRASSE

Gleimstrasse

PRENZLAUER BERG

WEDDING

SPREE

TIERGARTEN

MITTE

REICHSTAG

Strasse de 17. Juni

Unter den Linden

TIERGARTEN

HOTEL KEMPINSKI

KREUZBERG

SPREE

Kurfürstendamm

TOPOGRAPHY OF TERROR

NEUKÖLLN

BERLIN

and wanted to hand it all over to me to deal with. I was happy to agree to this, eager to find out more and to engage with this building that embodied some bit of what our family was, a place where it had belonged, something pre-dating the dispossession. And if it could result in money for my mother, so much the better.

So I began a long correspondence with the lawyers and agencies. It turned out that, between them, they were laying claim to more than 80 per cent of any final value. This came from the various percentages to be deducted – by the lawyer in Israel for having tracked down my mother, for the lawyer he appointed in Berlin to handle the negotiations, to the Jewish Claims Conference for handling the transaction, and to the German government to cover mortgage payments and repairs or maintenance that it claimed to have paid for between 1934 and 1990.

I was infuriated by these percentages and deductions. I saw a swarming horde of ruthless opportunists grabbing at the potential value of the building. Further complication came from a bogus claimant suddenly appearing, saying that the building belonged to them – though we could never find out who 'they' were, and I came to suspect that it was part of some nefarious dealings all too close to the Claims Conference. At the same time, the Claims Conference insisted that its rules dictated that the property had to be sold and the value thus shared; there was no question of the building being handed over to my mother, even with various liabilities. Nor was there any question of being compensated for the loss of some fifty-eight years of rents on those thirty apartments.

It looked as though this windfall would turn out to be a fascinating progression towards the return of close to nothing, and just a new reminder of all that my family had always wanted to forget. I was filled with indignation. It was unjust, unreasonable. These letters, the ever more perplexing tangle of facts and claims, made it look to me like another version of the 1934 dispossession, a reminder of layers of abuse, this time in part being effected by a Jewish organisation, under the aegis of the new, non-fascist Germany. By pitting myself against them all I could be at least some small distance inside the past, within relationships that centred on a building that was a piece of my family's history. I could make a great deal of noise, in that small space, that would break the silence.

On another visit to my mother I told her that I was determined to argue in every way that I could, and to bring any pressure I could think of, to oppose the percentage grabbers. I told her that we were facing another chapter of theft, another round of dispossession. Yet my mother was deeply uncomfortable with my indignation and resolve. Her response to the melting away of the asset under the great heat of others' demands for percentages was to shrug and say, in her inimitable way, 'I never knew about it so I expected nothing. Five pounds would be more than I could have hoped for.' I said that it was not only about money. There was an issue of principle, of justice. I urged her to agree with me that we should not sit back and let unjust fate take its course. She became more anxious, and kept saying that the one thing she knew was that to stir up the past in this way would bring sorrow, and that money of this kind coming into a family would lead to all sorts of trouble. So it wasn't worth it, whatever the value of that block of flats.

I knew that her response was touched with wisdom, but I felt that it was also part of her passivity by which I had always been troubled, and that it came from a very familiar set of fears. To challenge what was taking place would mean confronting a complex of faceless and remote authorities. Any such confrontation always filled my mother with dread, and caused her to be silent even in the face of obvious abuse of her rights. She could rage and be open in her anger at home, in herself, but not towards the outside world, where she always felt unsafe, on sufferance. Huge psychic energy went into her being acceptable and accepted, into not causing waves, not making any 'difficulties'. And who knew what the difficulties would be if she were to challenge this array of lawyers, the Claims Conference, the new German state itself? Then there was a fear of something that she saw as unearned, unexpected, unplanned for.

And there was the problem of remembering. To get involved in this property, to imagine her grandfather deciding to buy it, then his losing it, and then his murder by the Nazis . . . This was to go down pathways of memory that she had closed and barricaded. To make her life in England she had needed to stay away from memory, or from memory that led in a direct way to history. The pain of it was too great. And to negotiate this claim, to be drawn into the questions of what entitlement she might have to a building that had been taken from the family by the Nazis, was to be back there, defining and therefore bearing the unbearable and speaking to the unspeakable losses. Better to let whatever it was, this flow of legalese and bureaucratic stuff, this role of claimant that had been thrust on her, take its course.

My mother's reasons for taking no action, her willingness to accept whatever some invisible authorities in Germany decided – all this was what, in the depths of me, I wanted to confront. I did not worry about the family, or about the implications of accepting this compensation. I was pleased to dig out and break open, through discovering everything I could about this block of flats in Berlin, both family stories and this one small piece of the history of our times.

So I engaged in careful and persistent arguments with them all. In this I found I had an ally in the Berlin lawyer, who shared my outrage at the percentages and apparent deceptions and obvious obfuscation. It turned out that I was not alone: hundreds of other potential beneficiaries in the flood of 1990–93 claimants were expressing their outrage at the way their assets were again being taken from them by the lawyers, new institutions and the representatives of the German state. Legal actions had been launched. Threats and protests had been made. There was much retreating from the most egregious percentage grabbing, and even some shifts on the part of the German state in its view of what it might be owed for having taken care of its stolen properties. I got the lawyers' total down to no more than 25 per cent; the Claims Conference down by about a half of its original demand; the German state to withdraw its demands altogether. In the end, it looked as though my mother would receive about £200,000. A huge sum to her, and enough to make a very large difference to her old age, and a great help to us all. Hardly the equivalent of the value of what had been taken – the block was worth several millions of pounds – but the settlement looked like an amazing windfall, for all that.

In the course of the negotiations, and out of my own curiosity, I had been a few times to Berlin and visited the lawyer. He was young, clever and easy to get along with. I had been able to go through documents as well as strategise with him, as each new complication revealed itself. At the final stages of the negotiations he asked that my mother come with me to Berlin, to sign the final documents and give her instructions about payment. She was uneasy; do we really have to go? Well, I suppose it is necessary; she always thought she would at some point have to see the lawyer in his office there. So we went together, my mother and I, for a two-day visit to Germany.

We flew in to Schönefeld airport, on the northern outskirts of Berlin. Our lawyer had booked a room for us at the Kempinski Hotel in the heart of the city, a short walk from his office. I was excited to be back in Berlin, but my mother was uneasy, anxious. Was travel making her nervous? Or arriving in Germany? We decided to take a taxi to the hotel. As we climbed into the car, the driver asked us where we wanted to go: '*Wozu?*' My mother sat heavily into the back seat. 'Tell him where we want to go,' she said. So I did. As we pulled out of the airport the driver asked if this was our first visit to Berlin. 'I haven't been here for many years,' said my mother, in English. The driver asked another question, having much difficulty with English. 'Translate for him,' said my mother. So, in my rather childlike German, I answered his questions. He was interested to hear that my mother had been before. When was that? Again, my mother replied in English; I translated. She spoke fluent German; still listened to German radio; it was her first language. But she would not speak it in Germany, or not on this trip; for the length of the forty-minute drive from airport to hotel, I interpreted for her. And thus it was for the rest of our stay.

When we arrived at the hotel we went to our very grand rooms. My mother wanted a rest. I took a shower. I managed to get shampoo in one eye. It was still sore and weeping when we went to find some tea. We sat in the Kempinski dining room, a little in awe of the self-conscious grandeur and pretensions to Old World elegance. I made some comment to my mother about our finding ourselves in just the kind of hotel where we would never stay. She demurred. This is the right place to be, she said. She had always heard about the Kempinski from her grandfather; he had always stayed here on his trips to Berlin. So she knew he spent time in Berlin? Of course, she said, he would tell her stories about Berlin. But nothing about buying a block of flats here? No, she said, he never talked about his business. He cared about his library, his collection of Judaica – these were the things she remembered. And his chess set, the one I had learned to play on and she had seen him play on. Being here at the Kempinski made her think about him, so of course it was right that we were here. Then she commented on my sore eye. Odd, she said, your grandfather had one very bad eye. Looking at you squinting like that makes me think of him all the more, and you were given his name. She had no more time for fantasies about reincarnation than I, but the coincidence sent a small shock wave through me. It was a reminder of how close this journey to Berlin was bringing us to much of what had happened to the family: a childlike, superstitious part of me felt as if we were walking on the ladder of history, making connections that carried risks. We were here to secure a gain that was compensation for loss. But to be here was to rediscover loss.

My mother showed no such superstitious feelings and, on the outside at least, no feelings of grief. She refused to connect with the history that was to be found on the streets of Berlin. We walked to the lawyer's office, two blocks along the Ku'damm, with its expensive stores and thick traffic. She noticed that the Meissen china shop was a short way along the street and suggested we go there – she owned some intricate and very remarkable Meissen figurines and was a great fan of old Meissen china – but she seemed to have no interest in going any further, any deeper, into Berlin. I suggested that after the meeting we visit the Meissen shop and then, perhaps, make a bit of a tour of Berlin. How about going to see the Reichstag building? Or walk by the Brandenburg Gate? 'Whatever you like,' she said, without much conviction.

The meeting at the lawyer's office turned out to be brief and very simple. He explained the way the claim had come about, the course the negotiations had taken, the causes of the delays, and asked us to sign the relevant documents. This would release the first tranche of the money. He could give it to us the next morning, in any currency we liked. No, said my mother, it would be alright for them to do a bank to bank transfer. She was not intending to hide the money away. Ah, said the lawyer, his clients sometimes liked to take cash, even if it was hundreds of thousands of euros. A glimpse or suspicion of shady dealings made my mother go very quiet. She felt out of place in all this, and had her own fears about taking money at all. She had told me again, on the way to the lawyer's office, that she feared that no good would come of it. And I, again, had assured her it was far less than her due and she had every right to accept it.

We left the lawyer's office and went to the Meissen shop, then by taxi to the Reichstag building. I had learned that visitors could take a tour there; the restoration and rebuilding had just been completed. What would she think about going inside? Seeing the place where Hitler had first taken power, and which the new Germany was remaking as its centre of government? 'If you like,' she said. But she did not want to do this, and was relieved when we discovered that the queue to get in was very long, too long for her to manage. We should find some lunch, she said, enjoy that, and then go back to the hotel. I realised that sightseeing in Berlin was a bad and painful idea. So we found a small restaurant, ate a simple lunch, and went back to the Kempinski. She did not go out again. I went for a walk, but had begun to feel some of the grief that must have been lurking very close to the surface of this trip, emerging from its concealment within my mother's psyche.

But she clamped down on it. Would not go into those streets. Turned away from it now as she had done for all her adult life. I was less able, or less determined, to keep the grief out.

I was the second generation, not a direct victim of the Nazis. So I could allow the feelings in, and, in some ways, wanted to let them in, wanted to know them; or was willing to accept that they could not be denied. So I made my way to what had been Prinz-Albrecht-Strasse, renamed as Niederkirchnerstrasse, where the Nazis and Gestapo had their headquarters. I passed a building where, the guidebook told me, the Gestapo had turned a large network of cellars into a dungeon of cells and torture rooms. This was where they took people they picked up for 'questioning'. It was here, on this street, that Reinhard Heydrich had set up the office for the management of concentration camps; here where the meetings had taken place, the planning had been done; where Eichmann must have walked every day, taking a stroll to a café for his lunch, a break from the demands of the office.

Much was destroyed at the end of the war by Allied bombs, but enough remained to remind. It was being turned into a museum, a complex memorial, the 'Topography of Terror'. I walked into a square alongside the main street; more buildings from the Nazi era were preserved there. Long and high and dark facades. There was no one else there, at the end of a winter's afternoon. I leant against a railing and wept.

TO END

Before the Canadian government imposed its rules about dealing with death, the Inuit did not bury their dead. The frozen ground in winter and the hard permafrost a few inches below the wet surface of the tundra even in the warmest part of summer make burial very difficult. Insistence on compliance with Canadian law and the modern digging of graves at the new Arctic cemeteries is just one of the many refusals at colonial frontiers to concede much to environment. In 'the old days', which lasted in some corners of the north until the 1960s, the dead were laid out on the ground, near to where they had died, and covered with a pile of rocks.

The first time I travelled far in the Arctic, and walked with an Inuit elder up a hillside to be shown the lie of the land and be told stories about where and how people had lived before they were pressed into the new government settlements, I saw a surprising number of bones scattered on a hillside. 'Caribou?' I asked, thinking this must be a place where hunters had made some kills or cached the bodies of animals to be able to collect them later in the year. Human beings, the elder replied. And he pointed out to me a scatter of rocks spread out over an area about thirty yards across. He told me the names of the two people who had died and been laid under rocks in that place, and explained his relationship to them. The bears and foxes pull the stones down, he said, to get at the bodies. On other trips I would see rock piles that were still intact, with the bones of a dead person held within their weight.

I was moved and impressed by this form of non-burial. It helped deal with the prospect of entombment, an imagined claustrophobia even in death. It also spoke to me of a natural flow of the dead onto the land where they had lived, soon becoming a part of it all, ending as a scatter of bones. Picked over by a bear or the local foxes, carried in pieces by ravens; a melting into the systems of life of the place. And then the encounters between the living who continue to travel over this land and the bones of the dead, the remains of their parents and grandparents. Continuity and stability of life, a remaining on the land of the ancestors, a fixity of home that can last for many generations, that might well reach back in an unbroken line of use and inheritance 'since time immemorial' – the legal term for forever.

That this should have such strong appeal is not hard to explain. Inuit, and other hunter-gatherers, have stayed on their lands without seeking to transform them, and have made linkage to those lands a core of their personal and collective stories. Their minds have been filled by the mass of knowledge they have needed to make their kind of use of all that is around them. They have nourished and been nourished by their territories. In their world, across their spans of time, there is no such thing as dispossession; there is no history of being a refugee, no flight to some distant land, no need to escape to where a new language must be learned and a whole new life begun. Here was the opposite to the heritage I had come from, the burdens of history I had to carry within me. When I lived there within this Inuit system of the past, I could see and feel an antidote – for me, as a person needing to breathe this kind of air, and for humanity, with its need to establish another way of living in the world. It was an alternative to all that so often and so mistakenly have been deemed to be the inevitable cruelties of the human condition.

Original sin, the inescapable fault lines running through something called 'human nature' – these, or versions of them, have been used again and again to justify the oppressive violence and injustices of our society. Here was irrefutable evidence that there is no such thing as that cursed human nature. Human beings are never perfect; they have the capacity and appetite for cruelty. But the real evil and cruelty to be found in the modern history of indigenous peoples come from the colonial attack upon all that they have and all that they represent.

———————

In the conquest and domination of colonial frontiers, whole ways of life are devalued and silenced; stories cannot be told. The same can happen in the shadow of genocide, when those who survive feel that they must not relive their trauma. The life of the mind is then cut off from a fertile and vital source, and is thereby cut off from itself. The silence of those who felt they could not or must not speak about what had happened to them is an uncertain, fractured and anguished refusal to tell the stories that need to be told; children of those who find themselves thus silent are not able to discover vital parts of themselves.

Death casts its own shadow, issues its own apparent call for more. If there is death in the air, created and put there by people, by the cruelties of history, it becomes a part of something called destiny. Life can be made tentative, uncertain, impossible to trust, by a fate that is your own because it was the fate of so many just like you, ahead of you. Mass murder causes the children of survivors to feel the proximity of death, or to hold it within them, all too close to the centre of their young lives. Thus shafts of grief could reach through to me even when there would seem to be only reasons for happiness. And thus, at one dark time, was I drawn to killing myself.

Thus has suicide in the north, as among indigenous peoples around the world, sent out its own fatal messages. More than a possibility, an option, an idea that is always ready to spring into an unhappy mind. In this way a high rate of suicide among the young takes its place among the signs and results of the accumulated abuses of the people of the Arctic, as in so many parts of the world.

Growing up without a secure attachment to heritage or place, being from somewhere that I was told was essential and yet must not be relied on, made me aware that I had been shaped by events that it is better not to know about, having as parents people who could not tell their most important stories to me – these were the contradictory and subversive conditions of my childhood, just as they are for so many indigenous peoples. Here was an identification that I could make with peoples who were living in colonial shadows. Here was the work that would take me to their lives, and that gave anthropology its appeal. I was never conscious of this overlap, this possible motivation for choosing a profession that was for me, for many years, a way of life.

As soon as I began to learn about the hunter-gatherer societies of the far north, I wanted to go there, to be there. I never thought that this was a way of finding a history that might parallel my own. On the contrary, the impulse seemed to come far more from an idea I seized upon that there, in the far north, I would be able to live with and learn from people who did not share my kind of history, people who in many and crucial ways were living beyond the destructive reach of colonialism, people who would still be telling and hearing their own stories, people who had not been forced into silence. I aimed to arrive in a territory that was beyond the colonial margins, outside the history that had delivered, and continued to deliver, so much loss and grief.

Long before I set off for the far north, I had found the socialism of a kibbutz in Israel. I experienced community and equality – a place in which to find some reconciliation of childhood confusion, a chance for a new, healing form of attachment. With its reframing of the past and urging of a new model for the future, this was a vision of collective recovery. But the kibbutz had to exist within Israel the nation-state, and alongside the dispossession of Palestinian families and communities. Looking back at my experiences there, especially after the Six Day War of 1967, I came to see that a colonial frontier was always at work within the Zionist project.

Then, almost ten years after leaving Israel, I went to the Arctic. Without quite knowing it, with an intuition as much as a plan, I was in search of those who could take me into their distinctive wellbeing; I sought to escape my background. I did escape, did find a way of life that had its own genius and beauty, that took its meanings from land and heritage as far removed as possible from my own. Memory, journeys, life on the land – people could take me beyond the reach, or at least the destructive invasions, of the south. But the north, being a colonial frontier, was a complex of old and new, Inuit heritage and southern intrusion. To live the routines of settlement life was to experience a degree of modernity, perhaps some of its worst aspects. So I could both escape and fail to escape. Just like everyone else.

When living within the hunter-gatherer way of being in the world, outside the framework of comprehension and damage that I had known, I seized on a much wider insight into the human condition. Once I understood that there were societies living without the need to transform the environment or overwhelm other peoples, I believed that here was where I needed to be. I was, of course, both right and wrong.

Without knowing it, I had headed towards places where there was the greatest vulnerability. These were peoples whose lands and life were at that very time being incorporated into the southern, Euro-Canadian mainstream, who, as they kept telling me, could no longer live as themselves, who were being forced into a new and extreme degree of silence. Their very distinctiveness, as hunter-gatherers who lived in small isolated communities, refused hierarchy, shared their produce, spoke a language that no other peoples knew – all that made them who they were also made them vulnerable. They were not able to resist many of the changes that were imposed; many were rendered mute by confusion and dismay. I was finding some of the very damage that I had most wished to get away from. I had travelled as far as I could to escape the shadows of destructive history, only to find myself once again very close to its darkness.

In the far north I learned about the accumulation of abuse that has brought the world to new and newly dangerous levels of inequality and environmental damage. A billion human beings live in the destitution of shanty towns, without security of reliable food or safe water. The transformation of the earth by changing climate is threatening multitudes of people with drought, tornados and flooding. These dangers are dispersed and yet are omnipresent. Abuse has precipitated these threats. I saw this first and with most clarity in the far north. The Inuit, like many societies at geographical edges and cultural margins, reveal what is happening at the centre. Their experience of abuse, and their entanglement in its repetitive cycles, revealed the world I came from for what it is, or was becoming. The despair and deaths among their young was, for me, for all of us, a global warning. They showed me what was at risk, what the damage was, what the dangers were.

Like many of the Inuit and other hunting peoples I came to know, I could begin to see that their life, my life, and the life of the earth itself, depended on their way of being and knowing, the link they made between human health and the land, still managing to prevail. The facts, as Anaviapik had said, have to be known and understood. They are the basis for any attempt to provide the meaning that life itself depends on.

———

My mother needed to establish and then sustain silence. But when she broke this silence, or when my grandmother spoke in whispers, they took me to things that had happened. Then they found themselves, as we all find ourselves, having to deal with the rewriting of the history, where the search for experience encounters the various needs to deny it. They did this to protect the young, yet, without ever wishing any such thing, they perpetuated trauma – and created the need for another layer of silence.

As I headed into distant frontiers I was again faced with silences, dispossession, further silences, and I found or was assigned a role, the marching orders I was given by my Inuit teacher Simon Anaviapik – to do all I could to challenge silence, prevent and redress dispossession. Thus I found myself making maps and films that would give a voice to some of those resisting loss, breaking silences, re-establishing themselves as people with rights to lands, entitlement to a voice, a place as citizens in the societies in which they found themselves. This was to do battle with the voices and arguments of racism and prejudice, which sought everywhere I worked to justify the oppression of peoples by reference to supposed inferiority that came from colour of skin or massive falsehoods about levels of 'development' or 'civilisation'.

I listened to salmon-fishing peoples of the North Pacific Coast describing the way their rivers and mountains had been taken from them in the name of progress. I went with hunters of the subarctic forests to see where their land had been seized by farmers and forestry companies and turned into places where all that the hunters and gatherers depended on had been destroyed. I stayed with indigenous families on the reservations and government communities into which they had been herded and confined. I visited villages in western India where tribal elders showed me where all that they owned and built – elegant bamboo houses, patchworks of fields, ancient trees planted for fruit or for shade – was due to be flooded by a huge dam. I sat in the homes of tribal families deep in the forests from which they were going to be evicted because some officials somewhere far away had declared that this was now going to be a 'wildlife sanctuary'. And I made many trips to the southern Kalahari and sat with men and women in their grass huts and shacks beside the dunes of the desert, and in the houses where Bushmen were living in the poorest of 'Coloured townships'.

In all these places, in multitudes of conversations, I listened to men and women, speaking with quiet dignity, often with a good deal of humour, sometimes in despair and anger, always searching for ways to confront and deal with the abuses they had suffered, and telling me how they were deemed to be trespassers in their own territories.

In a drawer at the side of my mother's desk, held together by a wide, tight elastic band, I found a small bundle of letters. They were still in their envelopes, and all with the same familiar handwriting. They were from my father to my mother, written in the winter and spring of 1939. The postmarks carried the dates. Love letters. At the top of each one was a day – suggesting that they were part of a stream. I took out the first one and realised I was very reluctant to read it. This was more than private, the most personal of written words that a person can hold onto. They would take me to my father's heart and his sexuality. Things that had been kept out of sight, out of any apparent possibility of mind, all through my childhood, all through my life. These were territories that I was not supposed to know – more than that, deeper: zones that were closed even to the imagination.

I hesitated, put the letters aside, left them as they were, in their small bundle. I kept thinking: this is not for my eyes. And then thought: but here is a chance to meet my father, to know him better. I had always known so little about him. So I read the first of the letters, quickly, with a sense of shame, squinting at the words from the side. I did want to know what my father would say, what he was like, who he was, as a young man in love. The letter was full of love, and passion. Longing, and worry about some possible misunderstanding. A hint of pleading, assuring his wife-to-be that they would be happy together. In one sentence he referred to his Jewishness, telling her that it was not the most important thing to him, less important than other ideas. Her being from an assimilated Viennese background must have been causing some difficulty between them, some doubt in her mind – or so he must have thought – about their being mismatched. But the shock of the letter came from the fierce and total quality of his love, his ability to speak of love with such force and belief. This was not the man I had known; who had never been able to say or write anything really loving to his children; who had never hugged us; who, when I was an adult, would cause me to smile by the way he shook hands with me when we met or said goodbye. I was startled and yet delighted to find, in these letters, in that sprawling handwriting that I had always known, such intensity of feeling. But I did not read any of the other five letters.

In the same desk, in a different drawer, I found a diary unlike any I have ever seen: it was started as a way for my parents, in the first weeks after their marriage, to share their lives and thoughts. A double diary, with both of them writing entries, each informing and responding to the other. A statement, a flow of statements, of total openness and intimacy. In fact, this diary project did not keep going for very long. After a spell of entries, they stop. Perhaps my parents switched to a different notebook. More likely the demands to which it gave rise, the kind of exchange it depended on and intensified, could not be sustained. In effect, this diary turns very quickly into a mixture of confession and argument – about whether or not they should have a child as soon as possible.

My mother declares that she is longing to be pregnant. There is nothing more important to her, now that they are married, than to have a child. His child. And a child now, as a way of dealing with, defying, the terrifying uncertainty that the world was facing. It was the summer and autumn of 1939. My mother knew what the dangers of the Nazi project could mean – she had lived through the invasion and occupation of Austria, had fled for her life. Europe was about to be engulfed in war. Now, before war and invasion, before the possible destruction of their world, while they were still together in a home that was safe, they should begin a family. She spoke of how much she longed for this, for a baby. For a family.

My father was against it. For the same reasons – war, total uncertainty: this was not a time to bring a child into the world. He planned to join the army, expecting to be a doctor with the British forces in Europe. He would be away for long periods, and there was a risk that he would not survive. Better that they wait until these dangers were behind them, and think of having a child, making their family, in the peace that would eventually come.

My mother opposed my father's reluctance with her longing for children, and a year later, in September 1940, my brother was born. Two more pregnancies were to follow. I was the youngest, born while the war still raged. The one effective defiance for my mother of the Nazi project was to give birth, to sustain and increase life. My father's letters and the impassioned dual diary were where I could discover that defiance, that insistence on love and procreation. A right to be in the world. I knew, because I had lived it, that it is the question marks raised over this right to be alive, this loss of faith in any territory of one's own, by which wellbeing is obstructed and undermined. And this denial of rights and territory allows death to have a means of prevailing.

Each community I have lived within experienced the entwined narratives of silence and dispossession. These relate to both the mind and geography, losses of heritage and expulsion from home. The European Jews who were able to escape the Holocaust, which bore down so forcefully on those who grew up, as I did, in the homes of the survivors; the Palestinians who lost their homes and land as a result of the creation of the state of Israel; the Inuit, like so many indigenous peoples, whose culture and territories were occupied and transformed by dominant southerners who saw Arctic homelands as a new frontier; the San of the southern Kalahari who had everything taken from them. To focus on this commonality of history and experience is to risk a sense of despair: I know the forces at work, so powerful, so deadly.

I write the last section of this book as the Covid-19 pandemic surges on, spreading deeper and with terrifying implications into the homes of those who live most crowded together, the most vulnerable. This includes many indigenous peoples. Some have been able to rely on isolation to be safe. Others are at great risk. And there is the continuing irony, the bitter paradox of development: the more anxious and urgent the economic concerns at the centre, the more destructive its actions at its frontiers.

My mother conceived and gave birth as the war unfolded. Their first home was damaged in a bombing raid in 1941. News of the mass murder and the camps began to reach her in 1942. She learned the worst in 1945. At what point she fell silent, at what time she realised that the deaths and losses were too many to bear, in what part of herself the trauma of the events that were the global parallel to her creation of family, the extent to which the external deaths took root in her internal life – these are things I cannot know. But the transmission of death, as well as the shock waves from its suppression, shaped our home. Thus, like so many who grow up in the shadows and fallout of such events, the trauma was passed on to me.

In the same way that Inuit perceived the world around them from before birth, I feel that I imbibed a sense of death, or a deep and fatalistic sense of loss, from inside my mother's womb. Some would say that the catastrophe of her history, of history itself, must have made its way, in some genetic modification that came from all that happened, through her placenta into the tissue of her children's bodies. So her anxious fears, her belief that the mortal enemies were always close at hand, and had to be kept away by constant vigilance, were programmed into me. She used some degree of invisibility, which is another word for assimilation, and a zone of silence, to keep her – and me – safe, and she had both to deny and disregard her dispossession. I had to find other ways of coping, other routes out of 'the valley of the shadow of death' – which my father often said was his favourite line from the Bible – and find my own way to 'fear no evil'.

———————

Knowledge of the countryside, collecting birds' eggs, immersion in another land offered an escape to elsewhere. Yet wherever I was – be it searching for a bird's nest, casting a fishing line out onto a river or travelling by dog-team across the Arctic sea-ice – sudden moments of unhappiness, surges of infinite sadness, would remain with me. Thus I learned when very young that joy can often be touched, lit up even, by shafts of grief.

When I looked back at them from the distance, from outside the geography and cultures where I had grown up, I saw some of the larger, impersonal causes of unhappiness. Standing in the land and thinking from within the mindset of hunters of the Arctic or salmon fishermen on the North Pacific Coast, the fields and woodlands of Europe appeared to me as a net in which everyone had been caught. I understood that agricultural systems had taken control of the land, transforming it in its narrow image, and that this disposition to exploit the earth by reshaping it was, in the long run, a human and environmental disaster. I also understood that forms of aggression, from a tendency to the violent disciplining of children to recurrent and seemingly inevitable wars of imperial conquest, were social and psychological realities that were spawned by a particular kind of economy. As were the extremes of inequality and acceptance of complex, oppressive hierarchies.

This view of the world reinforced the messages and preoccupations that I had absorbed in the earliest stages of life. The more I witnessed the ways in which capitalism and imperialism unfolded at their frontiers, the more I grasped how deeply embedded these were. The ideas of development and progress, dense with racism, were voiced repeatedly within both visions of and justifications for invasion of the lands and lives of indigenous peoples, and entailed the possible eradication, therefore, of alternative forms of the human condition.

These processes were so profound and widespread, deep within me and everywhere I looked, that I struggled to see how they could be resisted. The enormity of their combined force could, by removing all hope, make me become a part of the fatalistic acquiescence, if not acceptance, that they relied upon. If these economic and political realities called capitalism and imperialism are so universal, so entirely a norm, then they cannot be checked. No doubt our densely populated planet cannot be fed and at the same time saved by a mass adoption of hunting and gathering. Much of humanity has been drawn, step by step, into the systems of agriculture and industry that we have come to depend on, and which condition so much of the land and even the oceans of the world. It is very hard to find ways of rethinking and remaking these dominant realities, but everyone is at risk if the logic of consumption and growth is not challenged and rethought. I came to believe that all that was best in humanity depended on the alternatives, but all too often I could not imagine how the relentless destruction of the development frontiers could be opposed, and how its alternatives be put in place.

Yet I also learned that there was always resistance and opposition. Some of it has taken place in the quiet and privacy of the home and family: elders have spoken their languages, knowing that to speak their words is to affirm their place in the world, and have told their stories, which is to show their possession of their territories. Younger men and women in indigenous communities have taken what they have heard and learned and defied the outsiders' rights to dictate the terms of life and have challenged their claims to the land, their plans to invade or exploit the resources they could find. Some indigenous groups have managed to launch legal actions to assert their rights. Others have celebrated and revived egalitarian modes of life. Where capitalism and imperialism seek to establish economic growth and profits as the guiding principles, indigenous peoples around the world urge respect – for one another, for the land, for the future.

I was led into and formulated these forms of resistance – in everyday life, learning languages, being out on the land, absorbing what it means to show and receive respect, as a witness in court hearings, in essays and books that I wrote, in films I was able to make. As I worked on the pages of this book, I kept seeing in my mind's eye the sharp, focused expression of Anaviapik's face as he explained to me that he, and everyone else, took endless pains to teach me because they wanted me to speak for them.

At the time I felt the force of this, the meaning and obligation it carried, in relation to Inuit who needed to challenge the action and decisions of the southerners who had power in their communities. But the longer I lived and worked with indigenous peoples, the more I realised that Anaviapik had assigned me a much larger, long-term task. I was to join with him, and everyone, in challenging the forces that were threatening to wreck or appropriate everything that was of value – respect between people, caring for one another, the languages of those who lived in these places on the edge, and all knowledge they carry, and, above all, the land itself.

The paradigm set out by capitalism, the social and material order established at imperial and colonial frontiers, is justified with assertions of a particular set of ideas about what is supposed to be natural and inevitable. Assertions that are based on pseudo-science and inventions. This paradigm and the regimes that support it are, for now, powerful and dominant. But they are neither natural nor inevitable. I have heard a different kind of story, and listened to some of those most threatened, damaged and silenced by what is called progress and development. Capitalism and its colonial frontiers are just one version of humanity, causing and defending greed, racism, inequality and the constant drawing down and destruction of the earth itself. These are the agents of death, causing and relying on silence. Life depends on opposing them all.

ACKNOWLEDGEMENTS

Some years ago, when I first began work on this book, I was receiving the great benefits of a Canada Research Chair at the University of the Fraser Valley in British Columbia. In their supportive administration of that Chair and their unfailing friendship, I cannot give enough thanks to Brad Whittaker and Adrienne Chan. Huge appreciation, also, to Debbie Block for all her help at UFV.

From the earliest drafts onwards Gillian Stern has been an invaluable editor and adviser. Throughout the process, Merilyn Moos has been unfailingly generous with her insight and editorial skills; she has again and again helped me to see with something like her clarity.

Leslie Pinder, who tragically died in 2021, read both early and late drafts, giving her time, insights, editorial advice and vital friendship.

Julia Blackburn supported and inspired in the course of many long conversations about all the themes in this book, read early drafts, and gave wonderful editorial advice.

Very many thanks also for their willingness to read early drafts, and for their wise advice and patient and untiring support, to Theo Baines, Jonah Brody, Steven Brody, Lorraine Brooke, Betsy Carson, Penny Cherns, Arnold Cragg, Nancy Hannum, Ursula Owen, Mike Poltorak and Kirk Tougas.

Jeremy Noble offered to listen to me read an early draft to him, and was astonishing for his patience and thoughtful responses.

John MacDonald, Arctic and Inuktitut scholar, helped me to correct many errors along the way and was wonderfully generous with his time and enthusiasm. Kathleen Lippa, Canadian journalist and expert on the Ed Horne case, about which she has written in sophisticated detail, has given both support and detailed critical advice.

Heather Jarman has, once again, been a tireless and brilliant editor. And huge appreciation to Kalina Norton for her wonderful work on the maps.

Friends and colleagues have made invaluable contributions to this book by sharing thoughts and providing, without even knowing it, those fragile essentials – unexpected ideas and self-belief – that all writing depends on. Many thanks for this to Mike Brearley and Colin Browne. As also to the wonderful Bill Kemp, source of endless insight about all things to do with both the Second World War and the Arctic, who sadly passed away while I was still working on this book.

I owe every one of these individuals more thanks than I can express here for their amazing blend of editorial skills and generous friendship. They must know that the mistakes and confusions that have survived into this final version of the book are all my own.

I want to pay tribute to the many people in the Arctic, especially in Pond Inlet and Sanikiluaq, who were my generous hosts, inspirational teachers and amazing friends. I owe infinite appreciation and gratitude to the Anaviapik and Aragutainaq families; Simon Anaviapik and Lucassie Aragutainaq were brilliant teachers of language and just about everything else beside. Many thanks, also, to Peter Kattuk, Lottie Aragutainaq, Alice Aragutainaq, Tina Inukuluk and Rita Kunuk who were guides and mentors at crucial stages of my time in the north.

I also owe a debt of special gratitude to Christine Moore, who shared the first journeys to Sanikiluaq.

And special thanks to Walter Donohue and Anne Owen, my editors at Faber, Tamsin Shelton and Paul Baillie-Lane, who, with great skill, copy-edited and proofread the manuscript, and to my agent, Georgia Garrett.

My family has endured all the swings of mood that seem to be part of writing; their care and love have kept me sane and, I suspect, alive. And at the heart of my family, always giving love, my Juliet – thank you.